D0146428

REHABILITATION TECHNIQUES
Vocational Adjustment for the Handicapped

REHABILITATION TECHNIQUES
Vocational Adjustment for the Handicapped

James S. Payne, Ed. D.
Associate Professor
Department of Special Education
University of Virginia

Allen K. Miller, Ed. D.
Doctoral Fellow
Department of Special Education
University of Virginia

Robert L. Hazlett, Ed. D.
Senior Associate
Helix II Consulting Associates
Charlottesville, Virginia

Cecil D. Mercer, Ed. D.
Professor
Department of Special Education
University of Florida

HUMAN SCIENCES PRESS, INC.
72 FIFTH AVENUE
NEW YORK, N.Y. 10011

Printed in the United States of America
123456789

Library of Congress Cataloging in Publication Data
Main entry under title:

Rehabilitation techniques.
Bibliography: p.
Includes index.
1. Vocational rehabilitation. 2. Handicapped—Employment. 3. Rehabilitation counseling. I. Payne, James S., 1931–
HD7255.R43 1984 362'.0425 83-26561
ISBN 0-89885-159-9

Dedicated to

Clare W. Graves,
for theory

Jerry D. Chaffin,
for application

Lao Russell
for inspiration

CONTENTS

PREFACE

This book was created and developed on the premise that rehabilitation programs represent, to many handicapped individuals, the link that spans the gap between total dependence and livelihood. Its purpose springs from the philosophy that all honorable work has dignity and that a nation should afford all of its members extensive opportunities to participate in such a humanizing and worthwhile activity as work. In essence, each country needs to foster the development of its most precious resource—its people.

This book is divided into three sections. Section I, Developing Human Resources, begins with a discussion of rehabilitation. Maximizing human potential is recognized as a common goal of the total rehabilitation process. In order to aid human development, it was determined that persons in the helping professions must operate from a realistic theory concerning the nature of man. The theories of Riesman, Heath, Maslow, Shostrom, and Schein are reviewed and incorporated into a complete theory of man as developed by Dr. Clare Graves. Graves's theory is presented as a workable operational base for effecting rehabilitation. The rehabilitation counselor's job is discussed in terms of using Graves's theory to grow people. Finally, Graves's theory is presented as an operational base managers can use to get people to do their jobs and enjoy them.

Section II, Vocational Adjustment of the Handicapped, focuses on the practical skills needed for securing and maintaining vocational resources for the handicapped. Practical techniques are described that demonstrate how the rehabilitation counselor can survey the community for training and placement resources, develop and maintain these resources, and evaluate the adjustment of the client. A summation chapter presents a model that enables the counselor to evaluate the client in the work environment.

Section III, Assessment and Development, describes research supporting Graves's theory. Chapter 9 explains how assessment instruments were developed in identifying Dr. Graves's "Levels of Existence." Finally, in the last chapter the application and exploration of a practical assessment method is offered.

This book is specifically developed for use as a primary text for introductory courses in rehabilitation (e.g., Rehabilitation Techniques). Since the book does not use the traditional labels that categorize areas of exceptionality (mental retardation, emotional disturbance, etc.), it provides a noncategorical approach to special education and would be suitable for supplementary reading for introductory courses in special education (e.g., Survey of Exceptional Children). As a resource book it can be used by vocational counselors, special education teachers, school principals, directors and supervisors of vocational programs, employers, and work study personnel.

The authors wish to express specific appreciation to the three outstanding individuals to whom this book is dedicated. First, we are indebted to Clare W. Graves, Professor of Psychology, Union College, Schenectady, New York, for his theory of man and work. Graves's theory, in addition to influencing our thinking throughout the book, provided a foundation for Section I. We are indebted also to Jerry D. Chaffin, Professor, Department of Special Education, University of Kansas, Lawrence, Kansas, for his gift of applying ideology and theory to the real world. Chaffin's practicality makes the ideas contained in this book usable. Finally, we are indebted to Lao Russell, President of the University of Science and Philosophy, Swannanoa, Waynesboro, Virginia, for her inspiration. Her graciousness consistently generated renewed life into the authors.

Special acknowledgment goes to Linda S. Wilberger for editing and typing the manuscript. Without her conscientious, consistent, and diligent work, the manuscript would never have been completed. Special acknowledgments go also to several students in our classes whose suggestions were most beneficial. These include Dale C. Critz, Jr., Michael R. E. Carter, William D. Cooney, William F. Trinkle, Hosea L. Mitchell, and Robert M. Woodell.

Part I

DEVELOPING HUMAN RESOURCES

Chapter 1.

I HOPE THIS BOOK . . .

Several years ago I was hired as a vocational rehabilitation counselor, and I* can readily recall my first day on the job. I was assigned a case load of handicapped clients, and my major responsibilities were too numerous and varied to list. My duties ranged from providing transportation for dental services to evaluation of clients on jobs. New, green, young, excited, and somewhat nervous, I was introduced to the vocational rehabilitation staff. I was instructed how to fill out the travel form for reimbursement and where to put the coffee money. Next I was handed a multipage manual and taken to my own office. I opened the door to see a barren room, for it had been stripped of anything that resembled life. There was an empty metal bookcase that looked as if it had come from an army surplus warehouse. There was a green metal desk, a swivel chair, and a regular chair for clients and visitors. On top of the desk was a stack of

---

*"I" refers to the senior author.

client folders over a foot high. I was instructed to read the policy manual and find the clients.

"What do you mean, 'find the clients'?" I responded.

"The last counselor left unexpectedly and the first thing you need to do is find out who and where your clients are," I was matter-of-factly told.

This is what is referred to as preservice training. Although preservice training has improved somewhat over the past few years, I hope this book will help the reader to understand something about rehabilitation *beyond* the policy manual and stack of client folders.

I read the manual and was confused by many of its terms and codes, and I had never seen so many forms. There were big forms, little forms, pink forms, green forms, yellow forms, lavender forms, forms for purchasing false teeth, canes, wheelchairs, transportation—103 forms in all, not counting the sign-in and sign-out forms. I hope this book *doesn't* have many forms in it.

When I asked questions about the various forms, I was told that I probably would understand them better as I worked with individual clients. Talking about forms in and of themselves isn't very interesting or meaningful. However, if I had a client to work with and he needed some type of service, such as dental service, then the forms for securing specific services would acquire meaning. Therefore, I decided to do what I was told and go find a client. I picked the folder lying on top of the pile and chose this person to be my first client. After reading the folder, I decided to go to the restaurant where the client was listed as working. I pulled up to the restaurant in a state car and entered, to find I had arrived at a busy time. Since the manager wasn't available to talk, I decided to have lunch. After eating, I was approached by the manager, who informed me that the client had walked off the job 4 months ago. I hope this book will help counselors to understand business routine, *schedule,* and business thinking.

It took me 4 days to find the client. He was at home, unshaven, watching television, and feeling sorry for himself. He was living in a place that smelled like urine and looked like a pigsty. I hope this book talks about *people as they really are.*

Within a year under my counseling and guidance, this client was placed on, and walked off, five different jobs. I hope this book mentions something about *evaluation* and *training.*

I remember once driving around the block three times to build up enough courage to talk with a hostile employer. He was mad and he had a right to be. My client lost his temper and broke the front window in the store. I hope this book talks about *how to approach an employer.*

I once knew an eager counselor who placed six clients on jobs in one day. He thought he had really done something. During a follow-up session one month later, he couldn't find any of them—they all had been fired. I hope this book has something in it about *follow-up.*

I heard of a client placed at the local humane society to care for animals. During the second week he felt sorry for the caged animals and went around opening all the pens. There were dogs all over the county, and it took over 2 weeks to round them up. Yes, I hope this book talks about *people's feelings.*

I once placed a client in a lumberyard. His job was simply to remove boards of a certain length from a conveyor belt as they came by. This client was a hard worker and rarely said a word. I thought this was a perfect placement. The next day the young man's father informed me his son was upset and had said he would kill himself if he had to go back to that job another day! Stunned, I asked what had gone wrong at work. His father replied that his son had told him that every time he bent over to stack a board taken off the conveyor belt, his hard hat would fall off and the boards would keep going by him on the conveyor belt as he tried to put his hard hat back on. We solved the problem by showing the client how to adjust the hard-hat strap. I hope this book doesn't forget to talk about those *little things* that mean so much to the successful placement of a client in a new job situation.

I once worked with a client who had spent considerable time in jail for stealing bicycles. I took him to a grocery store to be interviewed for a job. Things were going fairly well until he spotted a bicycle shop across the street. I couldn't get his nose away from the window. He just kept muttering, "I want to work in a bicycle shop." I gave up at the grocery store, grabbed his arm, and quickly went across the street to inquire about a job in the bicycle shop. I don't know how, but the client somehow got a job that very day and worked there for several years before he was sent to prison for breaking into houses. You know, I hope this book really does talk about people, *all types of people*.

I have had clients hug me, laugh with me, cry with me, curse me, throw things at me, and spit on me. I have experienced joy and sorrow, success and failure. I have worked with clients I enjoyed seeing come into my office and I have worked with clients I enjoyed seeing walk out of my office. At times I really liked working for vocational rehabilitation and at other times I couldn't stand it.

This book was written for persons who are working with handicapped people, plan to work with handicapped people, or think they might be interested in working with handicapped people. This book isn't complicated or technical, but it is accurate and somewhat detailed.

When I was an undergraduate, I enrolled in a course on first aid. The instructor valued first aid and felt it was an extremely important subject to know as well as to apply. He didn't want the course to get the reputation of being easy, so he set out to complicate a rather simple body of knowledge. He accomplished this by devising some of the craziest tests I have ever seen. We had to memorize all the bones of the body. To test our bone knowledge he placed each bone in a cloth sack. He handed us sacks labeled *A* to *Z*, and we wrote on an answer sheet what bone we thought it was by feeling the outside of the sack. Later in the semester we had an objective examination on the first aid manual that called for straight memorization of all italicized words, headings, and phrases.

The instructor did everything possible to knock all the life out of the course. He succeeded in taking an important yet simple subject and making it difficult. Some people try to do the same thing with rehabilitation. We don't want to oversimplify vocational rehabilitation, but neither do we want to project that it is too complicated for the average person to understand.

After reading this book, you should know a little bit about rehabilitation services and facilities. You should know something about different types of people and ways to approach them. And you should learn something about acquiring, developing, and maintaining an employer's interest in evaluating, training, and hiring the handicapped.

We are not interested in reproducing a policy manual nor in describing the characteristics of various handicapping conditions. We are interested in talking about assisting handicapped people with employment and life. As we talk about clients, facilities, services, trends, techniques, and theories, it must constantly be kept in mind that we are talking about people, not things nor statistics. We are talking about real people—real people who need help.

Handicapped people are not to be abused, felt sorry for, or pitied. They are people just like you and me. There is a film called *Leo Beuerman.*[1] Leo was so handicapped he was described sometimes as "grotesque" or "too horrible to look at." He was small, weighing less than 90 pounds, and his legs were bent out of shape so he couldn't walk. He also had poor eyesight and was hard of hearing. Leo lived on a farm in Kansas. Somehow he learned to drive a tractor, and later he invented a hoist to raise himself onto the tractor. He also invented and built a pushcart that enabled him to move around from place to place. He used his hoist to get his cart on the tractor; then he would get on the tractor and drive to town. In town Leo would park his tractor, lower himself and his cart down to the street, get in the cart, and propel himself down the sidewalk to a storefront where he repaired watches and sold pencils.

The reason this movie had such an impact on me is that I can remember buying pencils from Leo when I was a kid in school. As a child I didn't realize how remarkable he really was. He just wanted to talk to people, work, and do his own thing.

---

[1]*Leo Beuerman,* Centron Educational Films, 1621 West 9th Street, Lawrence, Kansas (13 minutes, color).

He wanted to be self-sufficient and independent. Here was a man, deformed to the point that, for most people, he was repulsive to look at. However, he was more of an individual, freer and more alive, than most people. As he sold his pencils, repaired watches, and made small leather purses, he thought about himself, life, and others. He was quoted in his later years as saying, "I hope someday I will be able to help the poor." You know something, *that's* rehabilitation.

As we discuss theories about man and work, describe rehabilitation techniques, explain facilities and services, and suggest how to acquire, develop, and maintain employer participation and interest, it must be remembered that we are talking about people—real, live, warm human beings. Their faults, their frailties, and their weaknesses must not be allowed to overshadow their present strengths. Some handicapped people just need an opportunity, an even break; others need support, and still others need intensive care and treatment. This book is about people, rehabilitation, and life. Don't read it for facts and figures to memorize. Read it for understanding.

Chapter 2.

LIFE-STYLES OF HUMANITY

Conflicts between family members, tribes, and nations have existed throughout the history of civilization. Religious views, skin color, politics, and hair length are a few of the topics that have traditionally ignited battles in living rooms as well as across continents. These conflicts between persons are encountered in all walks of life. Myers and Myers (1973) acknowledged the widespread existence of these conflicts in our society by stating:

> Parents and teachers are sometimes distressed by the appearance and behavior of young people. Clergymen are finding more concern with the here-and-now than in the hereafter and government officials are encountering rebellion against bureaucratic constraints. Union leaders are losing control of their members, and athletic coaches are learning that Lombardi-like charisma and domination no longer assure obedience and commitment among athletes. (p.48)

This widespread conflict among people has generated much human suffering, ranging from death to the retardation of personal-social growth of many people. The majority of these conflicts may be viewed as resulting from the mixing of opposing value systems.

It is possible to discuss human adjustment to different values or belief systems at four levels: (a) intolerance, (b) tolerance, (c) respect, and (d) appreciation. Hate characterizes the intolerance level, and survival of the fittest is the trend that prevails. Intolerance leads to war and culminates in both human suffering and destruction. The tolerance level is the level at which the joining of human effort from different value systems to accomplish group objectives becomes possible. However, this participation in a group effort is often achieved at the expense of much emotional involvement. Persons at this level may appear constantly "uptight" or even "bent out of shape." For example, a person can tolerate a toothache and continue to function in a socially acceptable manner, but it does not mean the person is happy about it. An examination of persons who function at the intolerance and tolerance levels readily reveals that much mental and emotional energy is used up in either attacking or adjusting to different value systems. This type of energy waste can serve to retard the efforts of rehabilitation programs aimed at developing human resources.

Respect enables individuals with different values to function together to accomplish group goals and actually enjoy it. Fondness of others with different values is obtainable to a degree at this level. The appreciation level enables a person to become very fond of other individuals who possess values dissimilar to his or her own. Respect and appreciation represent conditions that are complementary to the development of human resources. In essence, it is possible to identify each of the four adjustment levels respectively with the words hate, dislike, like, and love.

Behaviorists have convincingly demonstrated that appropriate environmental conditions enhance human growth, and nonsupportive environmental conditions retard the development or restoration of human potential. Respect and appreciation levels are characteristic of healthy environments and may be achieved in two ways: All people can be developed to the point that respect and appreciation are inborn values, or people can be matched in their immediate environments so they are surrounded by values consistent with their own.

It is necessary that professional persons in the social sciences strive to respect or appreciate people with different values. Although it would be desirable to have all persons respect and appreciate diffrent value systems, a history of conflict suggests that this goal is not immediately attainable. Thus, it is important that educators, rehabilitation counselors, and other social scientists strive to achieve the alternative by directing people into environments compatible with their values.

The psychological matching of people and environments is a viable solution, but a problem arises when one considers that a theory of humanity is needed that enables social scientists to understand the values of people and make accurate predictions. People make certain assumptions about others; these assumptions operate as theory and affect how a person deals with his superiors, peers, and subordinates. The person's effectiveness depends on the degree to which the assumptions match reality (Schein, 1970). In essence, a theory of humanity is needed that provides a realistic framework to guide the delivery of education and rehabilitation services.

A substantial amount of literature exists describing studies designed to define the nature of humanity. However, as exemplified by Schein (1970), many of these studies come to conclusions suggesting that people are so complex they defy categorization. This conclusion appears warranted when a person considers only a small sample of studies or when one model of humanity is sought. For example, Schein, in searching for a view of man, documented the existence of three distinct types of man, which led him to conclude that the development of a theory was impractical because of the conflicting life-styles. It appears that Schein was looking for one level to represent a theory of man, and when one level did not suffice, he concluded that the complex nature of man could not be classified.

The remainder of this chapter will focus on examining a representative sample of investigations and theories about the nature of people and how they think and act. The purpose of trying to present these various theories is to develop a usable and functional theory about people. The goal of this functional theory is to provide a framework for effecting human growth and development of both handicapped and nonhandicapped individuals.

Studies on the Nature of Humanity[1]

In an effort to understand the nature of man, Riesman, Glazer, and Denney (1953) studied people's adaptation to the environment and suggested that individuals primarily change because of variations in social and economic conditions. They suggested the existence of three different directions of personality development which are characterized under the headings of (a) tradition-directed, (b) inner-directed, and (c) other-directed. Riesman, Glazer, and Denney acknowledged that every individual possesses some aspect of each of these dimensions but usually selects one as a predominant mode of behavior.

Tradition-directed people develop according to the demands, customs, and beliefs of their social group, especially those of their family. Since tradition-directed individuals are governed by rules and pressures of the group, their uniqueness is repressed or submerged. These individuals are usually located in preindustrialized nations or communities. The inner-directed person is guided by internal demands and desires and thus is not at the mercy of external forces, pressures, and sanctions. Although they are aware of and sensitive to the social norms and customs, inner-directed people realize that a modern mobile society requires a strong self-will or internal set of values. The other-directed person is governed by parents and social group membership; however, the number of relationships are considerably expanded beyond those of the tradition-directed person. They are sensitive

---

[1]Adapted in part from: Pratt, G. W., & Mercer, C. D. Self-actualization and beyond. Unpublished manuscript, University of Virginia, 1973.

to others, they adapt to a variety of social situations, and they are likely to join humane and charitable organizations such as the Peace Corps or VISTA.

Hershey and Lugo (1970) suggested a fourth direction to add to the idea of Riesman, Glazer, and Denney (1953). This fourth direction is that of the self-directed person and is characterized by the behavior of the self-actualized person. This person trusts his intrinsic guidance and is capable of directing himself.

Heath (1964) presented a study focusing on the characteristics and types of change of a Princeton freshman class. Selected students were observed throughout their college program, with results suggesting that there were basically four major groups; these are presented in Table 2-1 and are called *X, Y, Z,* and *A*.

Individuals in the *X* group are called Noncommitters and may be described as conservative, friendly, and noninvolved. They prefer to maintain neutral positions and avoid arguments. Heath (1964) referred to a person in the second group (*Y*) as a Hustler and described these individuals as very active, with a great need for achievement and success. Heath employed the terms "fighter" and "aggressor" to explain the Hustler's nature. Individuals in the third group (*Z*) are called Plungers. These individuals frequently overextend themselves and thus exhibit a moody impression to others. The Plunger likes to engage in talk, has a tendency to overreact, and does not like an orderly schedule. The ultimate objective of personality development is found in the *A* group, which Heath called the Reasonable Adventurers. These individuals have the ability to create situations for their own satisfaction. They are intelligent, independent, and humorous; they like close friends, tolerate different ideas from their own, and have many interests.

Schein (1970) discussed the nature of humanity in terms of the assumptions that organizations have historically made about humanity. He presented these assumptions in chronological order of their emergence and categorized them under four headings: (a) rational-economic individuals, (b) social individuals, (c) self-actualizing individuals, and (d) complex individuals. Schein documented the existence of each stage by citing observations

Table 2-1.
Heath's Characteristics of Students at Four Model Positions

	X *Noncommitter*	*Y* *Hustler*	*X* *Plunger*	*A* *Reasonable Adventurer*
Reactivity	Underreactive	Counterreactive	Overreactive	Appropriate
Common Defense	Denial	Reaction-formation	Apology, Restitution	Reasoning
Attitude to Self	Unstructured	Rejecting	Alternating	Accepting
Social Motive	To belong	To be esteemed	To be noticed	To communicate
Problem	Self-expression	Self-acceptance	Communication	Frontier
Impresson on Others	Bland Friendly Conforming Neutral	Aggressive Tough-minded Cold Ambitious	Scattered Direct Impulsive Moody	Independent Sensitive Playful Compassionate
Characteristic Utterance	Who me?	Yes, but . . .	Why not?	If only, then . . .

of how organizations have interacted with man to achieve their desired goals. The rational-economic view of people springs from the philosophy of hedonism (pleasure-seeking individuals) and claims that man calculates the behaviors that will enhance their self-interest and then responds accordingly. At the rational-economic stage the emphasis is on efficient task performance, and people's feelings are reduced to secondary concerns. Rational-economic individuals work for material things and respond to both intelligently administered hard bargaining and traditional reinforcers such as bonuses, prestigious titles, incentives, and increased power. Schein cited the Hawthorne studies as evidence in support of the social viewpoint of humanity. These studies demonstrated that the need to be accepted and liked by fellow workers is a viable incentive for people. Social individuals emphasize the needs of the person as primary and relegate task performance to a secondary concern. They are concerned with feelings, acceptance, and a sense of belonging and identity. Self-actualizing individuals seek to fulfill their potential and demand a certain amount of autonomy and independence. These individuals are self-motivated and self-controlled, possess highly developed skills, and have great flexibility in adapting to various circumstances. Schein introduced the complex individual as a combination of all the stages. Schein stated that people are too complex to be categorized within one viewpoint, and thus a complex theory of humanity should be adopted. In essence, this view indicates that a person is a mixture of all three viewpoints, and different styles emerge as environmental conditions vary.

Another approach to describing the psychological position of individuals is presented by Everett Shostrom (1968) in *Man, the Manipulator.* As illustrated in Table 2-2, Shostrom claimed that people are basically manipulators or actualizors, and the life-style of manipulators is a set of learned values and behaviors. The manipulator is described as both needing to control others and needing to be controlled by others. This individual often is artificial, unaware, and nontrusting of others. The actualizor, in contrast, is described as honest, aware, free, and trusting of others. An actualizor likes uniqueness, and is a loving person who likes to become involved in close, warm relationships. The ma-

Table 2-2.
A Comparison of Fundamental Characteristics of Manipulators and Actualizors

Manipulators	*Actualizors*
Deception (Phoniness, Knavery) Manipulators use tricks, techniques, and strategies. They play roles to create impressions. Their overt behavior is deliberately selected to fit the occasion.	Honesty (Transparency, Genuineness, Authenticity) Actualizors are honestly able to express their feelings, regardless of the nature of those feelings. They are characterized by candidness and genuinely being themselves.
Unawareness (Deadness, Boredom) Manipulators are unaware of the viable concerns of living. They have restricted awareness because they only attend to what they want to hear and see.	Awareness (Responsiveness, Aliveness, Interest) Actualizors are sensitized to themselves and others. They are aware of nature, art, music, and the reality of experiences.
Control (Closed, Deliberate) Manipulators approach life in a calculated manner. They appear relaxed yet are very systematic in controlling and disguising their motives from their competition.	Freedom (Spontaneity, Openness) Actualizors are spontaneous. They are the masters of their life and feel a freedom to express themselves and develop their potential.
Cynicism (Distrust) Manipulators distrust themselves and others. In essence, they do not trust human nature.	Trust (Faith, Belief) Actualizors trust themselves and others. They believe that people can cope with life in the here and now.

nipulator, on the other hand, likes to use others for personal reasons. People usually have some aspect of both the manipulator and the actualizor as parts of their psychological structure. Shostrom stated that "only when we are aware of our Manipulators are we free to experience them and derive from them actualizing behavior." (p. 12) As individuals gain awareness of their manipulations, the manipulations decrease and actualization increases. Along with this type of insight and awareness, Shostrom suggested that group dynamics activities may be helpful in the transformation of manipulation to actualization. He also suggested participation in actualization training, sensitivity groups, and marathon groups to aid in the development of the actualization process.

Maslow (1968) developed a system of hierarchical needs that parallel the growth of humanity. The needs of this hierarchy are listed in ascending order:

1. Physiological needs (i.e., food, water, oxygen)
2. Safety needs (i.e., security)
3. Belongingness and loving needs (i.e., affection, identification)
4. Esteem needs (i.e., prestige, self-respect)
5. Self-actualization needs

It is important to note that the lower-level needs must be met before the needs of the next level emerge. Insufficient satisfaction of needs at one level will keep the individual from developing to the next level and ultimately will stifle self-actualization. Although Maslow (1968) developed the hierarchy of needs, he dealt much more extensively with the self-actualized person than with those of lower need levels. He described this person as one who does not judge or interfere, one who possesses a tolerant attitude toward others. Maslow (1971) stated that self-actualized people tend to be unconventional, unrealistic, and unscientific. He claimed that few people ever reach this level and estimated that less than 1 percent of all people reach it. An important part of the task of self-actualization is "to become aware of what one *is*, biologically, temperamentally, constitutionally, . . . of one's capacities, desires, needs, and also of one's vocation, what one is fitted for, what one's destiny is." (p. 32)

In order to help individuals grow, it appears that their basic needs (the needs that people have in common with animals) must be met until they reach the level of self-actualization. Maslow

(1971) suggested that a clinician should help the client "to unfold, to break through the defenses against his own self-knowledge, to recover himself, and get to know himself." (p. 52) One of the main values of Maslow's theory is that it presents a comprehensive approach for human growth that spans several levels of existence. However, it is not accurate enough to predict behavior for each person.

Graves's Theory of Man[2]

A final approach, and one which may in fact include all the others, is presented by Clare W. Graves, and it is possible that Graves's theory of humanity may provide the precision needed in the social sciences. Graves (1970) used Maslow's theory as a base for a very well organized theory of how people grow and change.

Dr. Clare W. Graves, professor of psychology at Union College in Schenectady, New York, developed a viable theory of humankind using the multilevel need theory as a base. The best way to comprehend Graves's theory of man is to turn to original sources and to practitioners who use his theory. The following passages are taken from an unpublished manuscript entitled "Clare W. Graves' Theory of Levels of Human Existence and Suggested Managerial Systems for Each Level," compiled by the staff of the Management Center, University of Richmond (Richmond, Virginia, 1971).

> The theory advocates that the psychological growth of mature man is an unfolding process marked by the progressive subordination of older lower-level behavioral systems to higher-level behavioral systems. Each successive level is a state of equilibrium through which people pass to other states of equilibrium. At each stage the individual has a psy-

---

[2]Adapted from: Payne, J. S., Mercer, C. D., Payne, R. A., & Davison, R. G. *Head Start: A tragicomedy with epilogue*. New York: Behavioral Publications, 1973, pp. 126–139. Reprinted in part by permission.

> chology that is unique to that level. Actions, feelings, motivations, ethic values, and thoughts are all behavior manifestations which are required to deal with problems at a particular level. Also, persons at each level prefer a particular style of management. That is, in different levels of existence, an individual acts, feels, thinks, judges and is motivated through different managerial styles.
>
> A person does not mechanically grow to another level of existence. Constitutionally, he may not be equipped to change in an upward direction although the conditions of his environment change. A person may continue to grow, under certain conditions, through a systematic series of ordered behavioral systems or stabilize and live a life at any one or a combination of levels in the hierarchy. Thus, persons live in a potentially open system of needs, values and aspirations, but often settle into what approximates a closed system. In order for people and their societies to grow they must subordinate old values and behaviors to develop new values and behaviors appropriate to new states of existence. Develop and discard, retain and rearrange, seems to be nature's way of handling things. (pp. 1–2)

Graves (1970) indicated that there are at present eight major systems of existence as outlined in Table 2-3.

First Level of Existence: Reactive

A person at the first level is primarily concerned with staying alive. The physiological needs are all-important, and all energy is consumed in reducing the tension generated by these physiological needs. Virtually, it is a state of psychological nonexistence in which an individual is not aware of self and in which he exists purely as a reflex organism.

A person at level 1 is not capable of productive effort and is consequently unemployable. Usually these persons exist in infancy and in severe forms of senility. Most are located either in state mental institutions or listed on welfare as totally dependent cases. Although these individuals are few and unemployable in the United States industrial system, businesses that emerge or develop in underdeveloped countries must deal with them.

Table 2-3.
Hierarchical Development of Man's Forms for Existence, Motivational System, and Organizational Problems

Level of Existence	*Nature of Existence*	*Motivation*	*Organizational Problems at Each Stage*
8	Experientialistic	Experience	?
7	Cognitive	Existence	Contributing
6	Sociocentric	Affiliation	Acceptance
5	Manipulator-Materialistic	Independence	Prestige
4	Saintly-Conformist	Security	Stability
3	Egocentric	Survival	Survival
2	Tribalistic	Assurance	Creation
1	Reactive	Physiological	—

Second Level of Existence: Tribalistic

Second-level persons progress to a state beyond that of mere physiological existence. Their basic needs are for stability and safety, and they begin a state of psychological existence in which the brain awakens and receives stimuli but does not comprehend or understand them. Individuals at this level vaguely realize that they exist as individuals separate from an external world. They live lives that are strongly defended but not understood.

Magical thinking is ingrained in their existence and greatly influences the way they live. Safety is an overwhelming concern, and although they are basically passive, they will use force readily if they feel threatened. Tradition and ritualistic thinking provide them a means to assure their safety. People at this level are capable of productive effort, providing it does not clash with the superstitions and magical beliefs that guide their life-style. They are strongly influenced by tradition and power exerted by authority figures (i.e., boss, chieftain, teacher, policeman, etc.).

Third Level of Existence: Egocentric

Third-level persons become totally aware of their existence as individual beings. The higher brain processes begin to awaken as new stimuli thrust on their consciousness. They realize that they are alive and that they must die, and this fact triggers a survival need which is psychologically based. All external forces are immediately interpreted as threatening, and it is necessary to combat them through self-assertion. Existence at this level is characterized by competition, aggressiveness, and a morality of the "eye for eye and tooth for tooth" variety. Power is respected, and the best means of obtaining it is through rugged, aggressive, self-assertive individualism.

Egocentric-level people further realize they have the power to manipulate the world to the betterment of their existence and to the fulfillment of their self-centered survival needs. They readily insist that winners in this fight for survival deserve the spoils of their victories and that losers are relegated to a state of submissive existence. They also perceive that the powerful individual has the legitimate right to authoritarian control over the lesser individual or the "have-nots." It is important to note that the losers or "have-nots" in this system hold the same values as their authoritarian counterparts but are reduced to a miserable life of trying to beat the system.

Fourth Level of Existence: Saintly and/or Conformist

The reality of death encourages third-level individuals to question the reason for their existence since ultimately the powerful and the weak face death on equal ground. Why does an existence characterized by the reverence for power face such a powerless ending? The problem of death provides the incentive for third-level individuals to seek a new level of existence.

When individuals reach the fourth level, the inequality of earthly conditions is accepted, and the problem of death is resolved. To them there is an all-powerful external force that determines and guides the nature of each person's existence. The will of this all-powerful force provides the fourth-level person with a framework for establishing the guidelines for a saintly life that esteems sacrifice as a means to salvation. This sacrificial style of life manifests itself through actions characterized by denial, deference, piety, harsh self-discipline, and self-indulgence.

Fourth-level persons are very secure in their saintly way of life, which usually unfolds under the guiding authority of one of the world's great religions or philosophies. They thrive on rules, order, and moralistic prescriptions. It is worthwhile to note, also, that such individuals focus on the means (sacrifice) rather than the end (salvation).

Fourth-level people historically have presented a puzzling relationship between values and actions. Although the sacrificial existence is highly regarded, these individuals have fought many wars over whose sacrificial system will prevail. Myers and Myers (1973) described the fourth-level person as a conformist with low tolerance for ambiguity and for people with different values.

Fifth Level of Existence: Manipulator and/or Materialistic

When fourth-level people begin to question the value of the sacrificial life, they start fulfilling the conditions needed to move to the fifth level. These fifth-level conditions focus on living a life guided by the attainment of wealth and its associated pleasures. Fifth-level individuals feel a strong desire to be independent, and this independence is achieved by conquering the physical world through a positive, objective, scientific method that simultaneously enables them to collect wealth. Although both third-level and fifth-level people are concerned about conquering the world, they differ in their method. Whereas the third-level person uses force and power with reckless abandon, the fifth-level person rationally approaches the means and carefully avoids the wrath of others. The strong materialistic needs of fifth-level people are reflected in their value system, which respects competition, gamesmanship, and the business attitude. They seek higher status and strive to manipulate people and things.

Graves (1970) noted: "Fifth-level values improve immeasurably human conditions for existence. They create wealth . . . and lead to knowledge which improves the human condition." (p. 150)

This level represents the mode of existence for much of middle-class America. Although there are many persons who exist at this level, it is interesting to note that persons at the saintly level consider them somewhat sinful.

Sixth Level of Existence: Sociocentric

Sixth-level people have traveled through the hierarchical order of needs concerned with survival, safety, order, salvation, and material gain. Predominantly, they are concerned with social matters and seek a work environment that is pleasant. Sociocentric individuals strive to be accepted and liked. They are very sensitive to group standards, and their behavior always reflects that of their group. Level 6 persons are very flexible, and their behavior is predictable when viewed in conjunction with peer influence. They have high affiliation needs, hate violence, and are concerned with social issues.

The following excerpt from Graves (1970) assists our understanding of existence at this level:

> On the surface sociocratic values appear shallower, less serious and even fickle in contrast to values at other levels because the surface aspect of them shifts as the "valued-other" changes his preferences. But the central core of this system is a very solid process. It is being with, in-with and within, the feelings of his valued other. (p. 151)

Seventh Level of Existence: Cognitive

Seventh-level people have progressed from subsistence levels to levels of true *being*. They have achieved an existence free of needs that are common to animals. Their cognitive selves leap into freedom, and they dwell in an environment of abundant motivation where their concept of existence greatly broadens. They are uniquely human and have no fear of God, boss, survival, or social approval. They are confident of their ability to survive in any situation. They are intrigued with existence itself and dwell on the improvement of existence states of all beings. They are concerned with people as becoming and welcome any alternative that enhances existence. Persons at this level enjoy living for its sheer pleasure. To them the means, methods, or ways are relatively unimportant, but viable ends are extremely important.

Seventh-level individuals are high producers as long as the means to an end are left to personal direction. In addition to being producers they possess creative excellence. This combination makes them valuable resources in advanced technological and professional service fields.

Eighth Level of Existence: Experientialistic

When the need to esteem life is satisfied, people grow to experientialistic states where they realize that they cannot know all about existence. A problem-solving existence gives way to an intuitive existence level at which individuals must adjust to the reality of existence and accept what they can't explain.

They value wonder, awe, reverence, humility, fusion, integration, unity, simplicity, the noninterfering receptive perception versus active controlling perception, enlarging consciousness, and the ineffable experience (Maslow, 1968). They insist on an atmosphere of trust and respect, avoiding domination. They are end oriented and take their activities very seriously.

The life and work of Walter Russell as reported by Glenn Clark (1973) provide many illustrations of the type of thinking that is derived from meditation and is inherent in an eighth-level existence. For example, Russell stated:

> No greater proof than my experience is needed to prove to the doubting world that all knowledge exists in the Mind universe of Light—which is God—that all Mind is One Mind, that men do not have separate minds, and that all knowledge can be obtained from the Universal Source of All-Knowledge by becoming one with that Source. (p. 36)

AN INTEGRATED THEORY OF HUMANITY

A good look at the many theories concerning the nature of humanity certainly testifies to the complexity of the problem. Manipulators, actualizors, plungers, hustlers, inner-directed, other-directed, and conformists are just a small sampling of terms used to define the characteristics of people. However, a critical review of the theories reveals that an astonishing degree of similarity exists among them. To begin with, it is obvious that Graves's (1970) theory is the most comprehensive and expands a broader range of psychological existences than do any of the other theories. The span and framework of Graves's theory enables us to integrate all of the theories into a meaningful perspective.

As illustrated in Table 2-4, Graves (1970) and Maslow (1971) are the only theorists to incorporate the lower levels of existence (reactive, tribalistic, and egocentric). Although Maslow does not discuss the hierarchical stages in terms of different life-styles, it

Table 2-4.
Stages of Humanity: A Composite

Reisman, Glàzer, & Denney	*Heath*	*Schein*	*Shostrom*	*Maslow*	*Graves*
Tradition-Directed	Noncommitters			Animal-related needs Life-styles	Reactive Tribalistic Egocentric Saintly-Conformist
Inner-Directed	Hustlers	Rational-Economic individuals	Manipulator		Materialistic Manipulator
Other-Directed	Plungers Reasonable Adventurers	Social individuals Self-actualizing	Actualizor	Self-Actualization	Sociocentric Cognitive
					Experientalistic

is apparent that the existence of Graves's reactive person originates from a concern for physiological needs. The tribalistic and egocentric existence levels appear to spring from a combination of the physiological and safety needs presented in Maslow's hierarchical need structure.

Riesman, Glazer, and Denney's tradition-directed person and Heath's noncommitter correspond to the saintly-conformist level in Graves's theory. This level would originate from both the need to belong and the survival needs in Maslow's hierarchy.

Riesman, Glazer, and Denney's inner-directed person, Heath's hustler, Schein's rational-economic person, and Shostrom's manipulator are congruent with Graves's materialistic-manipulator level. The self-esteem needs in Maslow's theory would tend to produce a life-style similar to a materialistic or manipulative level of existence.

Riesman, Glazer, and Denney's other-directed person, Heath's plunger, Schein's social person, and Shostrom's actualizor are representative of Graves's sociocentric level of psychological existence. Also, it is reasonable to say that the social and self-actualization needs as identified by Maslow would provide the psychological foundation for the sociocentric level of existence.

Heath's reasonable adventurer and Schein's self-actualizing person are the only levels that extend to the cognitive stage that Graves (1970) describes. In Maslow's (1968) discussions of the self-actualized person he appears to mix the sociocentric level with portions of Graves's cognitive level. For example, the dimension of fear and the concern with means to an end is not present in the person functioning at Graves's cognitive level as it is in Maslow's self-actualized person.

Graves (1970) is the only theorist to incorporate the experientialistic level of psychological existence. It is possible that the popularity of this level is depressed because it is new and unique. According to Graves, "These eighth level experientialistic values are only beginning to emerge in the lives of some men." (p. 155) Moreover, Graves believes that if the proper conditions exist, eighth-level values will someday become the dominant value system.

The open-ended aspect of the theory is important to consider

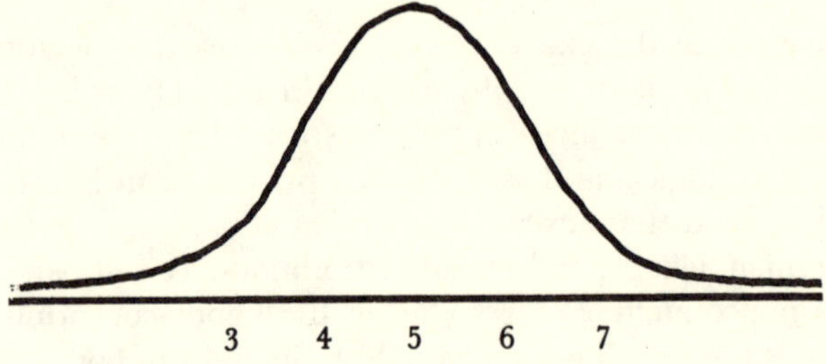

Fig. 2-1. Graves's open personality type at fifth level.

since Graves (1970) sees humankind continuing to grow into levels currently unknown. For the present, Graves stated, "And so we come, momentarily, to the end of man's value trek." (p. 155)

Many people have a tendency to reject the theory described by Graves (1970) because it appears to be categorizing people. However, it can be argued effectively that he is encouraging exactly the opposite. Our society is prone to judge by stereotypes that are, in actuality, grouping. For example, stereotypes exist for nurses, doctors, ministers, counselors, lawyers, teachers, policemen, and countless others. Graves reveals the illogic of this categorizing approach by demonstrating that all of these groups may contain a broad array of systems of behavior (i.e., conformist, materialistic, etc.). Furthermore, Graves (1972) acknowledged that approximately 95 percent of the people whom he has studied during the past 14 years operate at one level most of the time

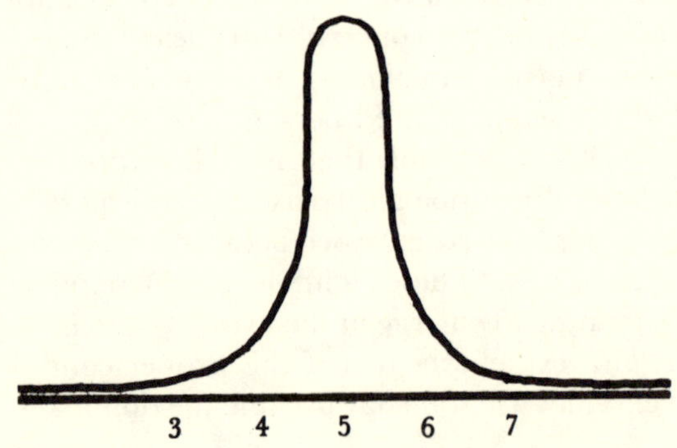

Fig. 2-2. Graves's closed personality type at fifth level.

but are capable of functioning at different levels under varying environmental conditions. As illustrated in Figure 2-1, Graves described these individuals as exemplifying an "open personality." In contrast, as illustrated in Figure 2-2, a small portion of the people he studied exhibited what he called a "closed personality." These individuals predominantly maintain the values of one level.

Conclusion

This chapter acknowledged that one of the aims of counselors and managers is to help individuals develop their potentials. The conflict of opposing values was presented as a problem that historically has not only generated human suffering but has retarded individual growth. Intolerance, tolerance, respect, and appreciation were discussed as a hierarchy of conditions that characterize an individual's adjustment to different values. Respect and/or appreciation were established as essential to a rehabilitation program. The existence of these conditions appears to be accomplished by (a) manipulating the immediate environment of individuals or (b) attempting to develop all people to more mature dispositions. The manipulation of the environment was determined to be a feasible goal for counselors, teachers, managers, and other social scientists. However, the logistics of an effective environmental manipulation is dependent on a viable theory of humanity.

The theories of Riesman, Glazer, and Denney (1953), Heath (1964), Schein (1970), Shostrom (1968), and Maslow (1968, 1971) were reviewed as a representative sample of modern theories concerning the nature of humanity. Graves's (1970) theory was presented as an all-inclusive theory, and the other theories were assimilated with it to formulate a simplified theory of humanity. It was implied that Graves's theory provides us with a composite of human beings that enables us to operate within a realistic framework concerning the understanding of values and the prediction of human behavior. The functional aspects of Graves's theory are demonstrated in the next chapter as intervention strategies for influencing life-styles are discussed.

References

Clark, G. *The man who tapped the secrets of the universe.* Waynesboro, Va.: The University of Science and Philosophy, 1973.

Graves, C. W. Levels of existence: An open system theory of values. *Journal of Humanistic Psychology,* 1970, *10,* 131–155.

Graves, C. W. Levels of human existence and their relation to management problems. (Brochure). Richmond, Va.: Management Center, Institute for Business and Community Development, University of Richmond, 1972.

Heath, R. *The reasonable adventurer.* Pittsburgh: University of Pittsburgh Press, 1964.

Hershey, G. L., & Lugo, J. O. *Living psychology.* London: Macmillan Company, 1970.

Management Center Staff, Institute for Business and Community Development, University of Richmond. Clare W. Graves' theory of levels of human esistence and suggested managerial systems for each level. Unpublished manuscript, 1971.

Maslow, A. H. *Toward a psychology of being.* (Rev. ed.) Princeton, N.J.: Van Nostrand, 1968.

Maslow, A. H. *The farther reaches of human nature.* New York: Viking Press, 1971.

Myers, M. S., & Myers, S. S. Adapting to the new work ethic. *Business Quarterly,* 1973, *38*(4), 48–58.

Riesman, D., Glazer, N., & Denney, R. *The lonely crowd.* New York: Doubleday, 1953.

Schein, E. H. *Organizational Psychology.* (2nd ed.) Englewood Cliffs, N.J.: Prentice-Hall, 1970.

Shostrom, E. L. *Man, the manipulator.* New York: Bantam Books, 1968.

Chapter 3.

INFLUENCING LIFE-STYLES

Rehabilitation counselors are constantly faced with the task of intervening in the lives of clients during crucial periods of development. Medical treatment, vocational evaluation, vocational training, job placement, and adjustment counseling represent some of the services that the counselor delivers or coordinates according to the individual needs of clients. Clients constantly seek help with vocational, social, and personal problems, and consequently counselors are often thrust into roles that require them to assist other persons with decisions that may, in effect, ripple through a lifetime. In order for counselors to manage the demanding task facing them, it is essential for them to (a) examine their own developmental profile, (b) acquire basic knowledge in the field of counseling, (c) understand the process of matching individuals with compatible environments, (d) decide on a growth or stabilization plan for clients, (e) develop prescriptive counseling skills, and (f) begin appropriate counseling strategies for each life-style.

PROFILE OF A COUNSELOR

An extensive list of desirable characteristics for counselors would be extremely long and undocumented in the empirical literature. However, awareness, acceptance, sensitivity, flexibility, and resourcefulness have been selected as the characteristics that appear to be essential in delivering counseling services via Graves's theory.

Awareness involves the ability to recognize the different existence levels of both clients and resource personnel. This recognition of individual life-styles includes using such observational cues as dress, nature of questions, nature of problems, nonverbal behavior, and language in order to determine the psychological existence level of persons with whom the counselor works.

Acceptance refers to the ability to respect or appreciate the values of others regardless of their dissimilarity to the counselor's personal values. Many counselors confuse acceptance with approval and thus limit the range of people they can work with on a mature level. Judgment does not need to be incorporated into the acceptance process. Personal values that necessitate the judgment of others may lead a counselor to impose values on clients that are not needed for the client's growth and development. It is unlikely that a helping relationship between counselor and client will follow unless they agree on the objectives that the relationship was formulated to accomplish. Counselors with intolerance for values unlike their own severely limit the range of objectives they can work toward and restrict the variety of means available to them for accomplishing given objectives. For example, if counselors are unable to tolerate long hair, it is unlikely that they can develop the relationship needed to accomplish counseling goals with a long-haired client.

Sensitivity incorporates a motivation on the part of counselors to advance the dignity of their clients. This sensitivity involves a self-directed responsiveness by the counselor to human problems that stifle growth and promote mediocrity. A mentally retarded client who seeks a job, a paraplegic who seeks vocational training, and an emotionally disturbed youngster who seeks to answer the question, "Who am I?" are examples of problems that should awaken the counselor's desire to respond enthusiastically. In essence, counselors should enjoy delivering rehabilitation services to the majority of clients whom they are charged with serving.

Flexibility consists of two main components: (a) the possession of a broad range of behaviors, and (b) the ability to shift psychological gears as the needs of clients vary. To illustrate, let us consider two clients, one mentally retarded and one an intelligent paraplegic. The mentally retarded client wants help with the problem of getting transportation to work. It is highly probable the counselor will respond in a very directive manner and do most of the talking. On the other hand, for an intelligent paraplegic client who is seeking help with a career choice, the counselor is likely to respond in a nondirective manner in hopes of promoting self-inquiry. Moreover, counselors may rely on the learning principles and techniques of behavior modification to cause behavior change in some clients but draw from humanistic strategies to promote growth in others.

It is likely that resourcefulness is the difference between effective and mediocre counselors. It entails the ability to locate, develop, organize, and coordinate services that aid the counseling process. It usually takes numerous services to complete the rehabilitation process. For example, physicians, visiting teachers, psychologists, employers, and many others often contribute to the rehabilitation plan of a client. Often the counselor's effectiveness is directly related to the ability to obtain and arrange the delivery of timely services. Extensive, well-organized files, associations with appropriate professional groups, and daily contact concerning employment situations are a few of the factors that enable counselors to develop and maintain their resources.

Knowledge Acquisition

The accumulation of knowledge embraced by the field of counseling represents the second major dimension along which the training of counselors may be viewed. This knowledge is usually obtained in academic settings and is organized under such headings as the nature of counseling, occupational information, abnormal psychology, small-group dynamics, and counseling techniques. In their training it is essential that counselors accumulate information and develop skills that enable them to draw from an assortment of counseling strategies (nondirective, directive, behavioral, and psychoanalytic) that may be employed to assist clients. These strategies provide counselors with both a theoretical reason why and a variety of approaches for accomplishing their job. The qualities of awareness, sensitivity, acceptance, flexibility, resourcefulness, and knowledge acquisition are not the only characteristics that make a good counselor, but they do represent the essential elements the counselor must possess to succeed in matching environmental situations to psychological characteristics for the purpose of aiding human growth.

Matching Individuals with Therapeutic Environments

A crucial feature of the rehabilitation processes involves the placing of individuals in environments that promote their growth. For most clients this process usually means placement in environments where the prevailing values are similar to their own. Although only a few studies concerning the matching of individuals to environments on the basis of values have been recorded, a review of these studies will be helpful in understanding the value-matching process.

Perry (1970) examined the development of Harvard and Radcliffe students over a 4-year period and developed the theory that intellectual and ethical development occurs in an orderly manner. This provided the framework for a nine-position theory of human development somewhat similar to Graves's (1970). Perry claimed that the nine-position theory allows teachers to effect "a differential address to individual students 'where they are'." (p. 210) He acknowledged two studies (Hunt, 1966; Wispe, 1951) demonstrating that the differential grouping of students according to developmental stages produced the expected results.

Students who received incongruent instructional procedures were less satisfied than students who received instructional procedures agreeing with their values.

Graves (1972) reported on an application of his theory in a large manufacturing organization. The intervention involved the placing of employees in positions where the task was congruent with their own values; it resulted in a 17 percent increase in production and an 87 percent drop in grievences. Also, plant turnover dropped in a year from 21 percent to 7 percent.

Myers and Myers (1973) have examined Graves's theory in a large industrial setting over a period of several years. Recently they suggested that supervisors and managers need to operate from a source of influence that does not produce conflict over values. In discussing this desired change, Myers and Myers (1973) claimed that today's successful manager "will be skilled in organizing manpower and material in such a way that human talent can find expression in solving problems and setting goals. He will know he is succeeding when the people stop fighting him, and show commitment in achieving job goals." (p. 51) In essence, Myers and Myers suggested that management should eliminate the conflicts existing between employees and employers by developing managers to a level that enables them to respect and appreciate the value systems of subordinates.

Two studies have instituted the matching of children with an intervention strategy on the basis of affective factors. A review of these studies serves to expand our perspective of the process of placing people in environments complementary to their lifestyles. Yando and Kagan (1968) used the Matching Familiar Figures Test to classify children and teachers as either impulsive or reflective. They reported that the children changed in the direction of the tempo of the teacher assigned to them. Since impulsivity is highly correlated to learning problems, a beneficial match was determined to be the placement of impulsive children with reflective teachers. Yando and Kagan indicated that the most dramatic results were obtained when impulsive boys were assigned to a classroom with experienced reflective teachers.

After 3 years of teaching hospitalized emotionally handicapped youths with learning problems at the Neuropsychiatric

Institute School of the University of California, Los Angeles, Hewett (1964) developed a hierarchy of educational tasks. The hierarchy consisted of seven levels that reflected the integration of psychological principles into a complete organizational framework for educators. In addition to outlining the characteristics of each level, Hewett described in affective terms the instructional circumstances appropriate for each level.

Counseling for Growth or Stabilization

Early in the counseling relationship, counselors must decide whether they are going to employ strategies that promote *intersystemic growth* or *intrasystemic growth.* Intersystemic growth refers to growth from one psychological level of existence to the next (e.g., a move from the conformist level to the materialistic level). Intrasystemic growth represents stabilization within a system (e.g., a conformist becoming a more mature person within the framework of the conformist values).

Intersystemic Growth

Blood, sweat, and tears frequently parallel the difficult growth process from level to level. This type of growth involves dramatic change and usually generates psychological conflict that may continue for long time spans. An examination of the conditions for intersystemic growth reveals the intense psychological processes that accompany humankind's developmental trek.

Graves (1970) discussed four essential conditions characterizing intersystemic growth:

1. An individual's needs at any one level must be satisfied to the extent that energy is released for exploration.
2. Dissonance or challenge must enter one's life at a time when needs at the present level are satisfied and surplus energy is available.

3. An individual must have an insight and become aware of human problems at another level.
4. Barriers (old values) to growth must be removed.

Solving the problems that exist at the person's present level allows the emergence of an excess of energy that can be used to think about the problems and ideas related to other life-styles. For example, at the tribalistic level, the individuals who have achieved a substantial degree of assurance and safety and who possess few problems of adjustment to the traditionalism of the tribe will discover that they have an excess of time and energy on their hands because things are going smoothly. This excess of time and energy provides them with the opportunity to question other things and expand their experiential existence. As Delamar (1972) pointed out, "he begins to think about what is going on around him; he begins to question tradition; but at this point, he is not dissatisfied with his lot." (p. 17)

Dissonance usually springs from a series of traumatic circumstances or disturbances originating from both external and internal domains. This conflict will generally serve to expose the shortcomings of the individual's present system. The realization of the present system's shortcomings, coupled with the excess of energy created by the first condition, heightens the possibility that change will occur (Graves, 1970).

The emergence of essential insights involves the recognition of values at the next level of existence. Awareness and adoption of the next-level values enable persons to resolve their dissonances and take a giant step upward.

A fourth condition that is usually necessary for intersystemic growth involves the weakening or removal of barriers (old values) that interfere with growth. These barriers exist in the form of confrontations with peers, family, and others who expect a continuation of the lower-level psychological existence. For example, as tribalistic-level persons move into the egocentric level, their behaviors become unacceptable to the people with whom they traditionally worked and lived. Barriers and confrontations result, and the continuance of the newly emerging life-style is determined by the person's dependency on the tribe and its traditions.

The conditions for intersystemic growth indicate that counselors take on a rather formidable task when they decide to promote it within a client. For the most part, rehabilitation clients seek assistance with maintenance-related needs, such as job, medical services, vocational training, etc. Generally, the fulfillment of these needs does not require a long-term relationship with the counselor and usually entails the improvement of a client's status within a particular level of psychological existence. Due to the nature of the problems that most counselors confront, the short-term duration of the client-counselor relationship, and the intense counselor-client relationship required for intersystemic growth, it is possible for the rehabilitation counselor to focus the majority of his efforts toward intrasystemic client growth.

Intrasystemic Growth

Intrasystemic growth involves a quasi-self-actualization process within a particular level. It involves living a life characterized by minimal conflict, and the expenditure of excess energy is usually accounted for in avocational pursuits such as hobbies and socialization activities with peers having similar values. Minimal conflict is frequently obtained by organizing one's life by ritualistic routines and living patterns; for example, work every weekday from 9:00 a.m. to 5:00 p.m., bowl every Tuesday night, play bridge every other Friday night, watch selected television programs, and so on. This example of intrasystemic growth may lead a person to assume that it is a life of drudgery and repetition, but it is important to remember that most of the individuals who have obtained a high level of intrasystemic growth are productive and very happy within their life-styles. Intrasystemic growth enables a person to stabilize and function within a restricted set of values. When viewed within a proper perspective, intrasystemic growth is a challenging and noble objective for counselors to adopt in most rehabilitation cases. Notable exceptions to the counseling goal of intrasystemic growth occur when a client's present life-style unjustly imposes on the rights of others or reduces the dignity of others. At this point it is worthwhile to note that these debilitating conditions may occur within the first six levels, but they almost always occur with reactive-level individuals, and frequently occur with tribalistic- and egocentric-level individuals. Finally, a high level of intrasystemic growth results from people being surrounded with value systems congruent with theirs to the extent that conflict is minimized and stabilization is secured.

Prescriptive Counseling

Because of the impact of environmental factors on the healthy development of individuals and the differential nature of therapeutic circumstances for respective individuals, it is essential that counselors recognize their existence as contributing environmental forces in the client's world. Not only should counselors avoid the tendency to consider themselves as separate from the client's world, but they should adjust themselves to the relationship in a manner that enables them to provide *prescriptive counseling*. Prescriptive counseling is a process that allows a counselor to provide counseling services tailored to the individual needs of clients. Simply stated, it involves diagnostic processes, the ability to plan and implement a strategy, and constant evaluation of both the accuracy of the diagnostic hypotheses and the effectiveness of the ongoing counseling services. Diagnostic goals usually include the assessment of three things: (a) the problem with which the client seeks help, (b) the level of psychological existence of the client, and (c) the design of a feasible counseling strategy. The implementation of the counseling strategy consists of coordinating the services of other resources and effecting a counseling approach—nondirective, directive, behavioral, self-control, and so on. Finally, evaluation is a continuous process and serves to monitor each stage of prescriptive counseling. Evaluation reveals the effectiveness or failure of the rehabilitation plan and provides the counselor with a reason for changing or continuing a counseling scheme. A discussion of the strategies appropriate for promoting growth at each existence level will serve to illustrate the counseling framework presented thus far in this chapter.

COUNSELING STRATEGIES FOR EACH LEVEL OF PSYCHOLOGICAL EXISTENCE

Reactive Level

The reactive-level person is not likely to appear in the case load of most rehabilitation counselors, but if one does, counselors should be able to develop an appropriate rehabilitation plan. The reactive-level person, with typical nonproductive existence, has a parasitic type of influence on the resources of a modern society. Not only do they sap the society of its vital resources but they fail to provide energy for its advancement. Because of the debilitating effects a reactive-level person has on a society, it is imperative for a counselor to design a plan that focuses on growing the individual to the tribalistic level of existence.

Intersystemic growth for the reactive-level person is achieved via a nurturant counseling process (Graves, 1972). As Graves (1970) pointed out, this type of nurturant counseling involves caring for the client in a mothering fashion. The nurturing process enables the individual to accrue a stable set of conditioned reflexes that provide automatically and dependably for the continuance of his existence. When the conditioned reflexes are established, the reactive person has gained entry into the tribalistic level (Graves, 1970). For many counselors it is not feasible for them personally to provide the mothering required by the reactive individual. However, the providing of nurturance does not require professional personnel but may be administered effectively by nurses' aides, volunteer workers, and ward attendants under professional supervision and guidance.

Tribalistic Level

Although tribalistic-level persons tend to come from preindustrialized civilizations, it is not uncommon for rehabilitation counselors to encounter them in ghettos or in disadvantaged neighborhoods. The tribalistic-level person is capable of productive work but only within a highly restricted environment. The work environment must be acceptable to the traditionalistic and magical thinking that tribalistic persons employ. If they think a condition in the work environment is inconsistent with their values, they will, at best, refuse to perform. An important factor to consider with tribalistic-level people is their severe reaction to values or situations not in accordance with their beliefs. Their reactions result from fear and are frequently manifested in violent action. Thus, a counselor should strive to promote intrasystemic growth in a client at this level only as long as the individual remains in circumstances that foster an existence similar to or congruent with the client's manifested life-style.

If clients are likely to be thrust into situations that are not complementary or supportive to their tribalistic way of existence (e.g., a migrant worker who is forced to settle near an industrial area), it is feasible to implement a strategy designed to facilitate intersystemic growth. A saturation of the tribalistic-level person's physiological and assurance needs would be the first objective of an intersystemic growth plan. A second phase of action would entail gradually exposing the person to brief encounters with egocentric-level values. This step would have to be taken slowly, carefully, and gradually in order to avoid severe reactions. The third phase of the plan would involve meshing the person into the egocentric-level society at a pace regulated by the client's adjustments. The removal of barriers to growth would parallel the third phase of the plan. This would involve removing the client from environments that promote the tribalistic way of life; for example, finding the client a job away from old friends, parents, and others.

Tribalistic-level people achieve intrasystemic growth by succeeding in fulfilling their physiological and assurance needs. The means for achieving this success must be congruent with tribalistic values. The means issue is crucial to the counseling strategy employed for persons at this level. The counseling strategy employed with tribalistic-level clients has three components: (a) modeling for evaluation of values, (b) modeling for skill acquisition, and (c) maintaining task performance via conditioning. In order to determine if clients are agreeable to participating in growth-related tasks (i.e., do a job, receive a physical examination, etc.), it is necessary for them to watch a model perform the task and then be asked to imitate the model. If the client attempts to copy the model, the task does not conflict with his value system. Once he agrees to perform the task, the second component can begin; this consists of learning the task by continuing to copy a model's behavior. The third component involves regulating the performance of the client through conditioning processes. For example, in a job situation the counselor would determine if the job were acceptable by demonstrating the job tasks and seeing if the client copied them upon request. If the client can imitate the counselor performing the task, then the counselor can have the client learn the task by imitating a model over and over.

It is apparent that the counseling strategies discussed for the tribalistic-level person do not involve much verbal interaction and are very directive. However, the effectiveness of these directive strategies depends on how well the counselor understands the client's way of life. Most of this understanding must be extracted from keen observation of nonverbal cues. An accurate assessment of the client's values and way of life enables the counselor to determine (a) the characteristics of the model to be used (female, male, tall, etc.), (b) the appropriate time for client exposure to the model, and (c) the types of behavior to be modeled. Also, it is important for the counselor to remember that the tribalistic person is essentially a nonverbal individual who is highly influenced by models. This requires that counselors be very aware of themselves as models and function in a manner that enables them to enhance the growth of their "eyeballing" client.

Egocentric Level

The egocentric-level client, like the tribalistic-level individual, is usually encountered in disadvantaged societies and is capable of living a productive life when handled properly. However, if dealt with improperly, he is apt to use ruthless force to exploit the situation for his own egocentric survival needs. Thus it is imperative for a counselor to employ counseling strategies that require the egocentric-level person to function in a desirable manner.

Since egocentric-level persons admire the power ethic and are capable of creating a society characterized by fear and insecurity, their destructive passions are controlled only by forces more powerful than their own. Thus, intrasystemic growth is justified only when it is likely that the egocentric-level client will exist in an environment dominated by a powerful force, which in turn supports the healthy advancement of society. Because of the problems with securing and maintaining a powerful authority figure who enables the third-level client to function for the betterment of mankind, it is often feasible for the counselor to adopt intersystemic growth goals for the client at this level.

An intersystemic plan for growth with egocentric-level clients would entail: (a) satiating their survival and power needs, (b) introducing dissonance by presenting the problems of the saintly level, (c) stimulating insight concerning the reality of fourth-level problems, and (d) removing barriers to the development of insight and growth.

The satisfaction of survival and power needs could be obtained by placing clients under a powerful force (employer, probation officer, counselor in residence, etc.) who constantly monitors their behavior while simultaneously guaranteeing them survival (job, food, protection, etc). After the intensity of the power and survival needs is lowered, the client has energy available to confront some problems of the saintly-level person's existence. The presentation of these problems is usually spearheaded by discussions concerning death. When it is pointed out to the egocentric-level person that everyone, no matter how powerful, has to confront death, the egocentric person may begin to recognize the fallacies of the egocentric power ethic. Then, via insight and reduced growth barriers (e.g., removing them from the influences of an egocentric-level family and colleagues by placing them on a highly supervised night job), they begin to question the reason for their existential problems: Why was I born? Why can't I find some success in life? Questions of this type as well as questions concerning the reason for the "haves" (affluent) and the "have-nots" (poor) impel the egocentric individual toward a quest of that ordered form of existence that assures a panacea. A quest of this nature places the egocentric-level person at the gate of the saintly level of existence.

If the counselor had reason to believe that the egocentric-level client would continue to live in an environment where the client's hostile aggression would be held in check without damaging effects on the client's existence, the counselor could justify an intrasystemic growth plan. This plan would focus on providing for the client's survival and power needs both on and off the job. The job would usually be physical (construction work, for example), highly structured, and supervised by a powerful force, such as an ex-Marine sergeant or professional athlete. Recreational activities would be designed to encourage the sublimation of aggression. Organized sports such as boxing, wrestling, football, and basketball would be healthy outlets for aggressive energy. Also, the possession of powerful motorcycles, leather jackets, customized cars, and power insignias (tattoos) facilitates the release of the egocentric person's aggressive urges. The counselor of an egocentric-level person should operate from a power position in order to be effective. It is essential to approach the client as hard-nosed, calloused, and extremely smart because the egocentric-level client will exploit situations characterized by the sociocentric ethic. Finally, this hard-nosed power approach, moderated by reasonable compassion and sensitivity, must be exercised in order to bring many of these individuals to life-styles that contribute to the survival of their respective societies.

Conformist Level

Rehabilitation counselors encounter many conformist-level clients in their case loads. Although conformist-level individuals are referred from all social class levels, they are most often lower and middle class. As mentioned in Chapter 2, these clients value structure, rules, authority, hard work, and sacrificial pursuits. Much of the credit for the accelerated rise of the United States is due to the contributions of hard-working persons at the conformist level. In our society many conformist-level persons achieve a high degree of intrasystemic growth because our democratic ideals enable them to worship as they desire, and the capitalistic aspects of our society enable them to work as hard as they please. Thus, intrasystemic growth is usually a feasible goal for the rehabilitation counselor to embrace with individuals at this level.

In order to be effective and to promote intrasystemic growth with the conformist-level client, the rehabilitation counselor must assume a counseling approach that is directive, structured, and highly organized. Counselors also should be sensitive to their clients' religious or philosophical values and not argue or confront them with the irrationality of their espoused values. In seeking a vocational placement for the conformist-level client, the counselor should look for an authoritative employer whose employees have well-designed roles and constant supervision.

Within the behavior modification domain, conformist-level individuals may be viewed as persons who primarily perform to avoid guilt. Persons on this level have an internalized punisher (superego) generating guilt that usually springs from religious values to shape the person's behavior. These self-inflicted punitive measures are often triggered by expressions of displeasure on the part of an authority figure whom they revere. Positive reinforcement from revered authorities (counselors, employers, ministers, government officials, parents, etc.) motivates them because they usually feel guilt for not deserving the reinforcement in the first place. In other words, they strive to think and act in accordance with the expectations implied by authority figures whom they respect and admire.

Materialistic Level

The case load of a rehabilitation counselor consists of many clients who function at the materialistic level of existence. This level represents the mode of existence for most middle-class Americans. The materialistic person's competitive nature and desire to perform in a manner that brings possessions and prestige have traditionally operated to advance the general welfare of society. The freedom and capitalistic structure that exists in our society enables the materialistic-level person to achieve intrasystemic growth. In essence they have the freedom to choose and change jobs or start their own businesses as means to materialistic ends.

To be effective with a materialistic-level client, the counselor must be perceived by the client as a highly skilled professional. The materialistic-level individual responds to a directive style of counseling as long as it is administered in both a firm and fair fashion. The client responds to rules, role descriptions, and policies that are formulated by respected authority figures and enforced in an objective fashion. In essence, the client at this level responds to reason (hard bargaining) and respects mastery and power.

Within a behavior modification framework, the materialistic-level client may be regarded as at the first level in the hierarchy that primarily responds to the positive aspects of reinforcement. Whereas the tribalistic, egocentric, and conformist individuals perform primarily to avoid negative consequences, the materialistic-level person performs primarily to gain positive consequences, such as money, prestige, or power. Thus, a prime rationale for the counselor to use with a materialistic-level client is to explain the rehabilitation plan in terms of materialistic values; for example, "If you receive this type of vocational training, you will be able to pursue a career that allows a person to advance quickly while making a good salary."

Sociocentric Level

The sociocentric-level individual usually emerges from a middle- to upper-class environment and is found frequently in the case loads of rehabilitation counselors. These individuals are characterized by their humanistic concerns, such as ecology, population growth, ill effects of capitalism, human feelings, self-actualization, poverty. Sociocentric-level individuals have certainly contributed to the general welfare of society by spearheading movements designed to reduce human suffering and increase people's sensitivity to one another. The sociocentric-level individual is highly motivated to participate in intrasystemic growth plans. Moreover, the sociocentric person frequently stabilizes at this level because growth from the sociocentric to the cognitive level is extremely difficult. The move from sociocentric to cognitive is the most difficult transition to accomplish as compared to the other level transitions.

Sociocentric-level clients, unlike the previous levels, respond to nondirective counseling techniques. They seek to understand feelings, explore alternatives, and share experiences with the counselor. Because the sociocentric-level client resists directive counseling, authoritarian bosses, and highly structured task-oriented environments, the counselor-client relationship needs to be very client centered. Clients on this level seek jobs that enhance personal growth and tap their emerging resources. Motivation on the job originates from the interaction of their valued peer group. As long as their peer groups have objectives that are compatible with the organization's objectives, sociocentric-level persons will perform adequately. The meshing of level-6 objectives with organizational objectives is accomplished by (a) working in a helping profession (nursing, mental health, education); (b) working with people (receptionist, counselor, operator); and (c) working where a high degree of enthusiasm exists among fellow employees. Also, the composition of the valued peer groups does not need to be exclusively groups of sociocentric-level individuals. The sociocentric ethic itself enables the person at this level to suppress his own needs for group purposes, thus enabling him to mesh with a group whose values reflect a different level. However, it is true that sociocentric persons will aggregate when enough are present.

Within behavior modification perspectives, sociocentric persons are a problem. They do not respond well to threat or traditional rewards (money, prestige, etc). They are concerned only about the consequences of their behavior as it relates to the welfare of mankind and their valued peer group. However, it is possible to consider the sociocentric person within the behavioral pattern by realizing that they perform for opportunities to engage in social interaction and activities that foster human development.

Cognitive Level

Because of their sophisticated survival skills and scarcity, cognitive-level individuals are not likely to be found in the case loads of rehabilitation counselors. Nevertheless, a counseling strategy with cognitive-level persons would consist of the counselor explaining the services that can be provided and then allowing the clients to select those needed to fulfill their goals. Individuals on this level resist demanding relationships and insist on handling their own growth or rehabilitation plans. In essence, the counselor offers services and delivers them on request. Although this counseling strategy appears to put the counselor at the mercy of the client, it would not operate that way. Cognitive-level persons are very mature individuals who respect the counselor. They would not jeopardize the counselor's position unless they thought the counselor was unfit for the job and damaging to the dignity of the client. Finally, if the counselor were at the cognitive level, it is possible that a close relationship would develop and be characterized by insightful discussions concerning the existential problems of humanity.

Experientialistic Level

Because of the extreme scarcity of experientialistic-level persons and their lack of concern with earthly problems, they would not appear in a rehabilitation counselor's case load. It is possible they would be referred by persons concerned with their intactness, but they would never agree to participate in a rehabilitation plan.

At the conclusion of this brief presentation of Graves's theory as applied to a rehabilitation counselor's job, it is important to reflect for a moment. As noted in Table 3-1, it is readily apparent that counselors must operate from a very sensitive and flexible posture. At one moment they are directing and telling; yet, at the swing of a door, they are reflecting, supporting, and sharing;

Table 3-1.
Counseling Strategies for Each Level of Existence in Graves's Theory

Graves's Levels	*Counseling Strategy*	*Motivation*
Reactive	*Nuturant Treatment*	External
Tribalistic	*Modeling* Force Negative Reinforcement Primary Reinforcers Directive	External
Egocentric	*Power* Negative Reinforcement Directive	External
Conformist	*Structure* Negative Reinforcement Directive	External
Materialistic	*Reasoning—Bargaining* Positive Reinforcement Directive	External
Sociocentric	*Nondirective* Democratic Group Counseling	External
Cognitive	*Facilitative* Nondirective	Internal
Experientialistic	*Support* Nondirective	Internal

and who knows, the next entry might stimulate meditation and self-inquiry. Graves's theory motivates us not to label people but to respond to them in a prescriptive manner. The theory illustrates the fact that in order for people to grow it is necessary to operate within their value system. Myers and Myers (1973) recognized this in their concluding remarks concerning managers:

> Value conflicts . . . can be ameliorated only by learning to operate from a new source of influence. Level 4 or 5 managers tend to operate from influence derived from official authority and tradition. To succeed with the new work ethic, they must operate from a base of influence stemming from the competence of people at all levels of the organization. (p. 58)

In addition, it is helpful to consider a point Graves (1972) made during a seminar. He implied that effective counseling does not necessarily depend on a theory of humanity but on resourcefulness and sensitivity to feedback. Resourcefulness entails the mastery of a variety of counseling strategies, and sensitivity to feedback involves the capacity to evaluate the appropriateness of the strategy and change it when it is not working.

Conclusion

Included in this chapter was a discussion of six major areas organized under the following topics: (a) profile of a counselor, (b) knowledge acquisition, (c) studies about matching individuals with therapeutic environments, (d) counseling for growth or stabilization, (e) prescriptive counseling, and (f) counseling via Graves's theory.

In a discussion on the profile of a counselor, awareness, sensitivity, acceptance, flexibility, and resourcefulness were featured as the essential characteristics of an effective counselor. Knowledge accumulation was presented as a factor that enables the counselor to develop an extensive pool of strategies. Selected studies concerning the matching of individuals to beneficial environments were reviewed from two perspectives: (a) adults in working environments, and (b) children in school environments. Counseling for growth or stabilization was discussed in terms of intersystemic growth (changing levels) and intrasystemic growth (within a level). Although it was concluded that intrasystemic growth was a feasible objective for most rehabilitation clients, it was pointed out that intersystemic growth is required for clients who do not promote the healthy advancement of society. Prescriptive counseling was presented as a process that involves (a) a diagnostic phase, (b) the ability to plan and implement a strategy, and (c) the constant evaluation of the accuracy of both the diagnostic and intervention phases. Counseling via Graves's theory was presented to provide the counselor with a framework for effecting prescriptive counseling. In conclusion, the reader was encouraged to recognize the application of Graves's theory as a means to stimulate and maintain the growth and adjustment of individuals with vocational and social adjustment problems.

References

Delamar, W. Graves and behavior in the work system. Unpublished manuscript, May 1972.

Graves, C. W. Levels of existence: An open system theory of values. *Journal of Humanistic Psychology,* 1970, *10,* 131–155.

Graves, C. W. Levels of human existence and their relations to management problems. (Brochure). Richmond, Va.: Management Center, Institute for Business and Community Development, University of Richmond, 1972.

Hewett, F. M. A hierarchy of educational tasks for children with learning disorders. *Exceptional Children,* 1964, *31,* 207–214.

Hunt, D. E. A conceptual systems change model and its application to education. In O. J. Harvey (Ed.), *Experience, structure and adaptability.* New York: Springer, 1966.

Myers, M. S., & Myers, S. S. Adapting to the new work ethic. *Business Quarterly,* 1973, *38*(4), 48–58.

Perry, W. G., Jr. *Forms of intellectual and ethical development in the college years.* New York: Holt, Rinehart, & Winston, 1970.

Wispe, L. G. Evaluating section teaching methods in the introductory course. *Journal of Educational Research,* 1951, *45,* 161–186.

Yando, R. M., & Kagan, J. The effect of teacher tempo on the child. *Child Development,* 1968, *39,* 27–34.

Chapter 4.

THE MANAGING OF PEOPLE

Persons interested in assisting handicapped individuals in rehabilitation need to be familiar with employer and business thinking. Life-styles of people and how to influence these life-styles have been discussed in the previous chapters. Here we will discuss traditional administrative theories through a historical perspective and dovetail people's life-styles with types of administrative structures. Most conversations about administrative theory concern how to get the job done. In this chapter we will discuss the assumptions and implications of two traditional administrative theories as well as how they relate to Graves's theory.

THEORY

In essence, a theory about humanity serves three functions: (a) to make sense out of chaos, (b) to assist in predicting behavior, and (c) to facilitate behavioral change. A theory of humanity takes the complex inner workings of human actions and makes some sense out of them—they did that because of a deflated ego or they did that because they are not getting reinforced enough, and so on. As the theory begins to clarify why people behave in a certain manner, it begins to predict—if that continues, they will quit, get mad, withdraw. A workable theory not only helps to explain and predict behavior but also suggests ways to change behavior, ways to get people to behave differently—if we do this, they will do that.

Most administrative theories make some assumptions about people, life, and work. Based on these assumptions, a system of management is developed to get employees to work toward job objectives. If individual employees do not fit into the system, they are usually fired.

The strength of a theory of humanity rests on its ability to explain, predict, and control human behavior. The strength of an administrative theory rests on its ability to get people to do the job.

One of the most effective ways to get people to do their job is to directly tell them what to do and then pay them to do it or punish them when they do not do it. This type of management is referred to as directive or authoritative management. This predominant management system is described by McGregor (1960) as Theory X. Theory X is based on the following assumptions:

1. Average people dislike and will avoid work.
2. Therefore, people have to be forced, controlled, and directed to work.
3. People prefer to be directed and have little ambition.
4. People seek only security.

Based on these assumptions, a Theory X work environment exemplifies structure and control. Managers are authoritarian and they constantly stress the directive and control functions of management. Rigid working hours, evaluation forms, corrective measures involving punishment, absolute authority and explicit role definitions provide the nucleus of tools for a Theory X mode of operation. Theory X managers must often exhibit that they are knowledgeable about the jobs of their workers. It is desirable that their workers feel that without their supervisor's guidance and knowledge their performance would drop to unacceptable standards. This dependency relationship with the manager enables the manager to gain the control that is so important in a Theory X work environment. Dependent workers strive to please their bosses and diligently avoid their wrath. To these employees "hell hath no fury like a boss's wrath."

Many well-known organizations stress Theory X or some modification of it as their managerial style. The United States Army is an excellent example of Theory X management. The army thrives on punctuality, policy, rules, structure, control, punishment, and the ranking system. All these tools characterize a Theory X management scheme. Public education is another well-known institution that has, for the most part, functioned on Theory X assumptions. The teacher is an authority figure and students are the subordinates. Tests, punishment, rigid time schedules, highly structured activities, and control devices are used today in most schools.

Although Theory X administrative thinking has been with us for centuries, it was first popularized by Frederick Winslow Taylor. Taylor became a pillar in industrial management around the turn of the century, and his impact on management is prevalent today. He worked with Bethlehem Steel Company in Philadelphia and is considered to be the father of "scientific management." Knezevich (1962) explained:

> The era known as that of "scientific management" did much to improve production and profit, but man was looked upon more as a producing machine than a personality. Through scientific study it was hoped that it could be discovered what positions, which hand, and what order of movement were to be followed by the "imperfect robot" called man, so that he might be a more efficient producer. It was not out of consideration to human qualities that better lighting, better heating, and ventilation were introduced in industry or business, but because the "imperfect robot" could produce

> better under certain conditions than others. The results of scientific management were less wasted effort and more efficient production in industry and government than ever before. (p. 105)

The reason for Taylor's impact on management was that he got the job done better, quicker, and for less money, and his popularity was enhanced through his writing style. Taylor's graphic descriptions of work situations are so real it almost hurts. Here is an example of Taylor's writing style explaining "systematic soldiering."[1]

> There is no question that the tendency of the average man (in all walks of life) is toward working at a slow, easy gait, and that it is only after a good deal of thought and observation on his part or as a result of example, conscience, or external pressure that he takes a more rapid pace. . . .
>
> This common tendency to "take it easy" is greatly increased by bringing a number of men together on similar work and at a uniform standard rate of pay by the day.
>
> Under this plan the better men gradually but surely slow down their gait to that of the poorest and least efficient. When a naturally energetic man works for a few days beside a lazy one, the logic of the situation is unanswerable.
>
> "Why should I work hard when that lazy fellow gets the same pay that I do and does only half as much work?"
>
> A careful time study of men working under these conditions will disclose facts which are ludicrous as well as pitiable. (pp. 19–20)

There is not a manager or working person alive who does not recognize the painful elements of truth projected here. Taylor was clever and explicit about the management of people. Here he talks about how he got Schmidt to increase his loading of 12½ tons of pig iron to 47 tons of pig iron per day.

---

[1]Taylor, F. W. *The principles of scientific management.* New York: Harper & Brothers, 1913, pp. 19–20, 42–47. Reprinted in part by permission.

Once we were sure, however, that 47 tons was a proper day's work for a first-class pig-iron handler, the task which faced us as managers under the modern scientific plan was clearly before us. It was our duty to see that the 80,000 tons of pig iron were loaded on the cars at the rate of 47 tons per man per day, in place of 12½ tons, at which rate the work was then being done. And it was further our duty to see that this work was done without bringing on a strike among the men, without any quarrel with the men, and to see that the men were happier and better contented when loading at the new rate of 47 tons than they were when loading at the old rate of 12½ tons.

Our first step was the scientific selection of the workman. In dealing with workmen under this type of management, it is an inflexible rule to talk to and deal with only one man at a time, since each workman has his own special abilities and limitations, and since we are not dealing with men in masses, but are trying to develop each individual man to his highest state of efficiency and prosperity. Our first step was to find the proper workman to begin with. . . . Finally we selected one from among the four as the most likely man to start with. He was a little Pennsylvania Dutchman who had been observed to trot back home for a mile or so after his work in the evening, about as fresh as he was when he came trotting down to work in the morning. We found that upon wages of $1.15 a day he had succeeded in buying a small plot of ground, and that he was engaged in putting up the walls of a little house for himself in the morning before starting to work and at night after leaving. He also had the reputation of being exceedingly "close," that is, of placing a very high value on a dollar. As one man whom we talked to about him said, "A penny looks about the size of a cart-wheel to him." This man we will call Schmidt.

The task before us, then, narrowed itself down to getting Schmidt to handle 47 tons of pig iron per day and making him glad to do it. This was done as follows. Schmidt was called out from among the gang of pig-iron handlers and talked to somewhat in this way:

"Schmidt, are you a high-priced man?"

"Vell, I don't know vat you mean."

"Oh, come now, you answer my questions. What I want to find out is whether you are a high-priced man or one of these cheap fellows here. What I want to find out is whether you want to earn $1.85 a day or whether you are satisfied with $1.15, just the same as all those cheap fellows are getting."

"Did I vant $1.85 a day? Vas dot a high-priced man? Vell, yes, I vas a high-priced man."

"Oh, you're aggravating me. Of course you want $1.85 a day—everyone wants it! You know perfectly well that that has very little to do with your being a high-priced man. For goodness sake answer my questions, and don't waste any more of my time. Now come over here. You see that pile of pig iron?"

"Yes."

"You see that car?"

"Yes."

"Well, if you are a high-priced man, you will load pig iron on that car tomorrow for $1.85. Now do wake up and answer my question. Tell me whether you are a high-priced man or not."

"Vell—did I got $1.85 for loading dot pig iron on dot car tomorrow?"

"Yes, of course you do, and you get $1.85 for loading a pile like that every day right through the year. That is what a high-priced man does, and you know it just as well as I do."

"Vell, dot's all right. I could load dot pig iron on the car tomorrow for $1.85, and I get it every day, don't I?"

"Certainly you do—certainly you do."

"Vell, den, I was a high-priced man."

"Now hold on, hold on. You know just as well as I do that a high-priced man has to do exactly as he's told from morning till night. You have seen this man here before, haven't you?"

"No, I never saw him."

"Well, if you are a high-priced man, you will do exactly as this man tells you tomorrow, from morning till night. When he tells you to pick up a pig and walk, you pick it up and walk, and when he tells you to sit down and rest, you sit down. You do that right straight through the day. And what's more, no back talk. Now a high-priced man does just what he's told to do, and no back talk. Do you understand that? When this man tells you to walk, you walk; when he tells you to sit down, you sit down, and you don't talk back at him. Now you come on to work here tomorrow morning and I'll know before night whether you are really a high-priced man or not."

This seems to be rather tough talk. And indeed it would be if applied to an educated mechanic, or even an intelligent laborer. With a man of the mentally sluggish type of Schmidt it is appropriate and not unkind, since it is effective in fixing his attention on the high wages which he wants and away from what, if it were called to his attention, he probably would consider impossibly hard work.

What would Schmidt's answer be if he were talked to in a manner which is usual under the management of "initiative and incentive?" say, as follows:

"Now, Schmidt, you are a first-class pig iron handler and know your business well. You have been handling at the rate of 12½ tons per day. I have given considerable study to handling pig iron, and feel sure that you could do a much larger day's work than you have been doing. Now don't you think that if you really tried you could handle 47 tons of pig iron per day, instead of 12½ tons?"

What do you think Schmidt's answer would be to this?

Schmidt started to work, and all day long, and at regular intervals, was told by the man who stood over him with a watch, "Now pick up a pig and walk. Now sit down and rest. Now walk—now rest, etc. He worked when he was told to work, and rested when he was told to rest, and at half-past five in the afternoon had his 47 tons loaded on the car. And he practically never failed to work at this pace and do the task that was set before him during the three years that the writer was at Bethlehem. And throughout this time he averaged a little more than $1.85 per day, whereas before he had never received over $1.15 per day, which was the ruling rate of wages at that time in Bethlehem. That is, he received 60 percent higher wages than were paid to other men who were not working on task work. One man after another was picked out and trained to handle pig iron at the rate of 47 tons per day until all of the pig iron was handled at this

> rate, and the men were receiving 60 percent more wages than other workmen around them. (pp. 42–47)

As can be seen in this illustration, Taylor knew his business. It is especially impressive that on two separate occasions he remarked that he not only wanted the job done, he wanted the employees to like it. Taylor was an expert at analyzing the task to be done, he knew the value of individualized instruction, and he used good reinforcement principles.

It is apparent that Theory X management is ingrained in our democratic society and in many instances deserves credit for advancing the country to its current status as a world power. Although many outstanding accomplishments have been achieved under Theory X, many problems have arisen as a result of it. These problems have culminated in the development of powerful unions, featherbedding, and open rebellion. Currently many employees are resisting restricting structure and tight controls. Townsend's (1970) statement, "And God created the Organization and gave It dominion over man" (p. 7), satirically represents the current rebellious spirit toward the organization.

The opposite of Theory X is Theory Y, sometimes referred to as humanistic management. According to McGregor (1960), Theory Y assumptions aboout humans and work are:

> 1. The expenditure of physical and mental effort in work is as natural as play or rest.
> 2. External control and the threat of punishment are not the only means for bringing about effort toward organizational objectives. Man will exercise self-direction and self-control in the service of objectives to which he is committed.
> 3. Commitment to objectives is a function of the rewards associated with their achievement.
> 4. The average human being learns, under proper conditions, not only to accept but to seek responsibility.

5. The capacity to exercise a relatively high degree of imagination ingenuity, and creativity in the solution of organizational problems is widely, not narrowly, distributed in the population.
6. Under the conditions of modern industrial life, the intellectual potentialities of the average human being are only partially utilized. (pp. 47–48)

Theory Y focuses on the basic goodness of people. It believes that an employee will function efficiently in a free environment, providing certain conditions exist. These conditions are based on the employee's need level and understanding of the organization's objectives. McGregor (1960) referred to Theory Y management as integrative management. That is, the employee's needs and the organization's objectives are integrated in a way in which organizational objectives become meshed with personal objectives. The reasoning is that if employees are instrumental in formulating organizational objectives, they literally interject their own ego needs into the objectives. Thus, involvement becomes the springboard for motivation. This integrative process is based on the premise that the psychological existence level of the employee is predominantly characterized by ego and actualization needs.

Theory Y operates through the following practices:

1. Employees participate in developing organizational objectives.
2. Employees and employers interact in problem solving.
3. There is a minimum number of policies and rules.
4. There is a lack of employee fear of management.
5. Employees are free to pursue organizational objectives.

6. Managers are not considered all-knowing.
7. Open communication exists laterally and vertically.

The basis of Theory Y thinking stems from a series of studies conducted at the Hawthorne Plant at the Western Electric Company in Chicago. The most comprehensive account of the Hawthorne Studies is reported by Roethlisberger and Dickson (1939) in *Management and the Worker.* This volume is lengthy, filled with details, and considered by management people to be a classic. At the college and university level, the Hawthorne Studies are often reported inaccurately. Many times a series of illumination studies are referred to as a part of or in their entirety as the Hawthorne Studies. Actually the illumination experiments were conducted during 1922 to 1927, prior to the Hawthorne Studies. The illumination studies, although not an actual part of the Hawthorne Studies, provided a necessary stimulus for the Hawthorne Studies and they are reported in the original Hawthorne report.

The illumination studies were composed of three separate experiments, all of which attempted to determine what effect the manipulation of light intensity had on production. The first study was conducted in three departments, and illumination was progressively increased. Production increased but was irregular and seemed to be independent of illumination. In the second experiment, only one department was used, and control and experimental groups were assigned. The results indicated production increased in *both* the control and experimental groups. The third experiment resembled the second except only artificial illumination was used and the light intensity was decreased rather than increased. Once again production increased in *both* groups. Since there did not seem to be any relationship between illumination and productivity, no interpretation was made of the three studies. An informal experiment was mentioned by Roethlisberger and Dickson (1939) about two workers involved in coil winding. These workers were placed in a locker room that could be made completely dark. At one point illumination was reduced to .06 of a footcandle, "an amount of light approximately equal to that of an ordinary moonlight night. Even with this very low intensity of light, the workers maintained their efficiency. They said that they suffered no eyestrain and that they became less tired than when working under bright lights." (p. 17)

The illumination experiments led the way to the Hawthorne Studies. The first of the Hawthorne Studies was conducted in the relay assembly room. The purpose of the study was to determine what effect rest pauses and length of the working day had on production. The task was putting a small relay assembly together. Six female employees were involved. The specific working conditions altered were length of workday, length and number of rest pauses, lunch program, and group-rate pay. Over a 3-year period, 13 separate conditions took place and production tended to increase. These increases in production were not attributed to any one experimental variable. It was noted, however, that the workers grew more friendly toward each other and they reported they liked the freedom of not being told what to do.

A second relay assembly group was developed to assess the importance of varying the wage incentive as a function of production. After approximately 16 weeks, it was concluded that not all increases in production could be explained by the wage incentive factor. Concurrently with the second relay assembly group, a study was conducted in the mica-splitting test room, where there was great variability in the workers' production, there was lower group spirit, and the workers never regarded themselves as special.

It was concluded from the three studies that the rate of production could not be attributed to the wage incentive system, improved working methods and materials, rest pauses, nor length of working day. It was felt that there was a need to study employees' attitudes. Employees' attitudes were examined through the use of interviews and counseling sessions. The employee-counselor discussions started out in a structured fashion and later were nondirective. The techniques used through the study were structured and unstructured interviews, observation, content analysis, and documentary records. Although Roethlisberger and

Dickson (1939) were not explicitly clear about the findings[2] of the original Hawthorne Studies, it seems clear to others in the field of management that workers bring with them many motives, needs, and expectations that influence the quality and quantity of their work and also affect their relationship to the organization (Schein, 1970). An oversimplification of a commonly accepted explanation of the Hawthorne Studies is that if employees feel important, feel cared about, or feel they are part of the organization, they will work harder and do a better job.

The term "Hawthorne effect," which is often referred to in educational literature, was first reported in *Research Methods in the Behavioral Sciences* (Festinger & Katz, 1953). An accepted definition of the Hawthorne effect is "a phenomenon characterized by an awareness on the part of the subjects of special treatment created by artificial experimental conditions. This awareness becomes confounded with the independent variable under study, with a subsequent facilitating effect on the dependent variable, thus leading to ambiguous results." (Cook, 1962, p. 118) In other words, people in experiments who know they are in an experiment do unpredictable things.

The whole idea about the Hawthorne Studies, whether in business, management, or education, is that people have feelings, and both individual and social treatments of humanity are very important variables.

Although organizations tend to adopt one theory or the other, it is apparent that both Theory X and Theory Y are very prevalent in management thinking. However, each theory in itself is not sufficient to explain the broad range of work behavior. Both theories account for a large segment of employee behavior, yet they are based on opposing assumptions about people and work. One claims that individuals are basically lazy, while the other insists that they are quite responsible. Since management style is basic to establishing functional programs, it is essential

---

[2]For an accurate yet concise description and analysis of the Hawthorne Studies the reader is directed to: Landsberger, H. A., *Hawthorne Revisited*, 1968. Order from: Distribution Center, N.Y.S. School of Industrial & Labor Relations, Cornell University, Ithaca, N.Y. 14850.

that a management model be adopted. Flipping a coin provides an easy alternative but leaves us victims of the chosen theory's inconsistencies.

Instead of choosing one theory it is possible to "have the cake and eat it too" by using both theories. Accepting both theories is feasible if people are viewed as different and changeable. In other words, some people are lazy while others are very responsible and energetic. Thus the assumptions that people are different, and that these different people are not static but changing, allows the acceptance of Theory X and Theory Y, depending on the basic nature of the individual employee.

The combination theory appears simple, but it must be remembered that occasionally individuals who are lazy break out of their pattern and emerge as basically responsible employees, while responsible individuals may regress to a state of basic laziness. When a boss decides to function on the basis of a Theory X-Y combination, flexibility in management style becomes essential. Some people need Theory X while others need Theory Y, and occasionally the same person will require a change in styles. The problem was described by McGregor (1960) when he noted that people with obvious ego and actualization needs function best under Theory Y and rebel under Theory X. On the other hand, he mentioned that people with high dependency needs function best under Theory X and become nonproductive under Theory Y.

GRAVES'S THEORY OF HUMANITY

In this combination Theory X-Y approach, the manager must constantly shift from one style to the other. It is self-evident that this constant shifting can be overwhelming without a basic operational model or strategy. The previous two chapters described and explained Graves's theory of humanity as a workable model. Graves's theory presents management strategies that stress both organizational production and employee growth, and it considers people as changing nonstatic individuals. The remaining portion of this chapter focuses on a brief description of each level and how a manager might handle employees at each level. Theory X assumptions and applications seem feasible for levels 1 to 5, and Theory Y is applicable to level 6.

First Level of Existence: Reactive

People at the first level are not aware of self or others. They are concerned only with the fulfillment of basic physiological needs. Graves (1966) explained this level of existence by incorporating individual's comments on their experiences at this level:

> My mind froze, grew numb, empty and dead, one is so tired, so utterly weary. Thoughts crawl. To think is such a labor and even the smallest voluntary act becomes painful to perform. Even talking, having to reply, get one's thoughts together, jars on the nerves, and it is felt as sheer relief to doze, to not have to think of anything or do anything. The numbness may indeed grow into a dreamlike state. Time and space disappear, reality seems infinitely far. (p. 121)

The suggested managerial style is a form of nurturant management. Nurturant management involves caring for individuals as a mother cares for an infant in hopes that it will grow to other levels.

Employers are not likely to deal with a first-level person as an employee. Persons functioning at this level exist in infancy or hard-core welfare cases and institutional cases.

Second Level of Existence: Tribalistic

Individuals at the second level live in a world of magic and superstition. They respond to tradition and the power of authority figures. The following description by Graves (1970) enhances our understanding of second-level.

> Causality is not yet perceived because man perceives the forces at work to be inherent, thus linking human consciousness at the deepest level. Here a form of existence based on myth and tradition arises, and being is a mystical

> phenomenon full of spirits, magic and superstition. Here the task of existence is simply to continue what it seems has enabled "my tribe to be." (p. 137)

Occasionally, people at this level are encountered as employees in an unskilled or semiskilled job. If they are not managed properly, they can present management with seemingly hopeless problems.

The appropriate managerial style to use with the second-level person is very restrictive and Theory X based. It is a style of management that is often referred to as a traditionalistic one. A manager must know the life-style of these people, understand their thinking, and be accepted in order to get them geared for work. Once they are amenable to working, their jobs are learned through imitating models that are presented many times by their boss. Thus, an appropriate managerial style would involve simple task demonstration coupled with the use of force to maintain production. However, Graves (1966) cautioned managers about the use of force since it only works when it does not conflict with a strong second-level taboo. If this conflict arises, second-level employees are likely to respond with forces of their own. At this stage Graves stated that cautious use of force works with second-level persons, but "*it will not work with first-level people.*" (p. 122) Hence, the need for different managerial styles becomes apparent.

Third Level of Existence: Egocentric

Third-level persons are rugged individuals who respect, admire, and respond to raw power. Graves (1970) discussed this level by examining their values and some conditions of their world:

> It is a world driven by man's lusts and is seemingly noteworthy for its lack of a "moral sense." But this is an error for at this level, where man is led to value the ruthless use of power, unconscionably daring deeds, impulsive action, volatile emotion, the greatest of risk, morality is ruthless.

> . . . This is not an attractive value system from other frames of reference, but for all negative aspects, it is a giant step forward for man. Some men, in their pursuit of power, *do* tame the mighty river, *do* provide the leisure for beginning intellectual effort, *do* build cities. . . . (p. 146)

It is possible that a large number of people in unskilled jobs and a few in semiskilled jobs exist at this level. They are potentially productive when managed correctly. If third-level persons are handled improperly, they will use ruthless force to exploit the business and fellow employees for their own egocentric survival needs.

Third-level individuals must be managed in an authoritarian manner. A manager must "out-power" these people in order to relegate them to a job role that involves taking directions and guidance. This style of management is called exploitative-authoritarian (Likert, 1967) and is unquestionably based on Theory X assumptions about humanity. Exploitative management, moderated by reasonable compassion and sensitivity, must be exercised in order to bring many of these persons to productive effort. Possibly, the more power needs the job role allows, the less power a manager would need to use. If one considers using an alternative management style, it is worthwhile to note that a Theory Y management scheme with third-level employees would be as disastrous as hiring a vampire to operate a blood bank. Under Theory Y, the program would be exploited and stripped of its humanistic function. Also, as has been pointed out by the staff at the Management Center, University of Richmond (1971), a supervisor would have great difficulty managing more than three egocentric-level employees at any one time.

Fourth Level of Existence: Saintly and/or Conformist

Fourth-level persons have low tolerance for ambiguity; they value rigid roles, rules, and policies. Individuals at the saintly level are typically motivated by religion, philosophy, or cause. Graves (1970) explains our view of fourth-level individuals in the following comment:

> He believes the task of living is to strive for perfection in his assigned role. . . . He believes that salvation will come ultimately, regardless of his original position, to he who lives best by the rules of life prescribed for him. . . . He who sacrifices best his wants in the way authority prescribes is most revered. (p. 148)

Fourth-level persons are often found in industry. They are found at all levels of employment from unskilled to professional. For example, they are prominent in the professions of education, ministry, law, and medicine.

The fourth-level person is most productive in a work environment that is highly ordered, structured, and organized. Managers of fourth-level employees must rigidly prescribe and rigidly enforce rules. This style of management is paternalistic in nature and is based on Theory X assumptions. Also, it is based on the assumption that some persons (managers) have invested responsibility to supervise the conduct of the managed, through parental-like concern. Likert (1967) referred to management at this level as benevolently authoritative. This manager is directive, firm, and authoritative, yet at the same time warm, sensitive, fair, and charitable.

Fifth Level of Existence: Manipulator and/or Materialistic

Fifth-level individuals value "cause and effect," objectivity, prestige, and material gain. According to Myers and Myers (1973), "they tend to perceive people as expense items rather than assets to be manipulated as supplies and equipment." (p. 51)

Fifth-level persons are found in all walks of life. These persons try to stay away from the more affective positions and professions such as ministry, social work, Job Corps, and so on.

Fifth-level people perform best under an autocratic style of management that is firmly but fairly administered. These individuals like matters to be handled in an objective fashion. It pleases them if job descriptions, job qualifications, performance evaluation, and job policies are clearly defined and objectively followed. They respect mastery and power and respond well to hard bargaining such as the "take name and kick tail" variety. They are motivated by systems that afford them equal opportunities to share in the organization's gains.

This style of management is called bureaucratic by Likert (1967) and resembles a very mechanical approach. Administration is accomplished via a steplike management system that functions according to well-defined rules, policies, and standard procedures. As with the appropriate managerial style for persons at levels 2, 3, and 4, it is based on Theory X assumptions about people and work.

Sixth Level of Existence: Sociocentric

Sociocentric persons dislike violence, tradition, and materialistic motives. They place high value on the dignity and worth of others. Their group behaviors resemble water being poured into a container. The water always takes the shape of the container, and level-6 persons' behaviors always reflect the behavior of the group of which they are part. From this analogy it is easy to perceive that level-6 individuals are very flexible, and their behavior is predictable when viewed in conjunction with peer influence.

The following excerpt from Graves (1970) assists our understanding of existence at this level:

> He values interpersonal penetration, communication, committeeism, majority rule, the tender, the subjective, manipulative persuasion, softness over cold rationality, sensitivity in preference to objectivity, taste over wealth, respectability over power, and personality more than things. (p. 151)

Sixth-level individuals are attracted to universities and are interested in service-oriented careers such as social work or counseling. They are interested in such programs as Job Corps, Head Start, Zero Population Growth, Humane Society, Weight Watchers, Rescue Squad. These people are truly concerned about helping fellow human beings.

Since sixth-level persons are democratically oriented and primarily concerned with social needs, the appropriate management style emphasizes group effort and employee participation in decision making. The management style for sixth-level employees is the first one based on Theory Y assumptions about people and work. The strength of this participative management depends on group standards and values. If sixth-level individuals fall under authoritarian-style management, the results are often disastrous. In this situation they will exhibit a classic display of passive resistance, and work performance will quickly tumble. Hence, to maintain an acceptable work performance, group management must prevail.

Level-6 individuals are many times looked upon by third-, fourth-, and fifth-level people as being nice but soft and weak. Therefore, level-6 persons are unable to manage lower-level persons adequately except for level 1. Persons at levels 3, 4, and 5 would manipulate and dominate a level-6 manager for selfish purposes. This domination results in level-3 people ruthlessly gaining more power, level-4 people demanding to follow rules and procedures, and level-5 people achieving small degrees of material gain through theft and devious ways. Meanwhile, the level-6 people continue their meetings and begin mumbling, "I don't understand why people can't get along because these people are basically good." Level-6 management will usually allow itself to be run out of business. Level-6 management can succeed with level-6 and level-4 employees providing there is no competition in their particular type of business. Although sixth-level persons do not possess the qualities and characteristics necessary for managing a business or program, they are invaluable in the area of service. They make good counselors, social workers, and teachers.

Seventh Level of Existence: Cognitive

Seventh-level people not only have high tolerances, but more importantly, they have an appreciation for people of differing values. Some theorists have referred to humanity at this level as self-actualized. Graves (1966) discussed some problems concerning seventh-level individuals in the following passage:

> He will not follow standard operating procedure. He will produce well—but only when the manager-producer role is reversed. . . . he rebels against the idea that it is management's prerogative to plan and organize work methods without consulting him, . . . management insists that he conform . . . he refuses. (p. 124)

Only a few seventh-level persons are found in business and industry. If a manager or administrator were fortunate enough to have a seventh-level person, it would be wise to consider an efficient and effective management approach.

Since they have much to contribute but refuse to be told how to do things, the appropriate management style is to achieve agreement on objectives with them and support them. This goal-oriented style of management would unleash their productivity, thus enhancing the organization's objectives. These persons could be dangerous administrators. Their intense desire to enjoy living might encourage them to view chaotic and hellish actions as intriguing and extremely enjoyable as long as they were purposeful. It would be similar to a manager standing off and observing the employees in an experimental box; and when things began to run smoothly the manager would shake the box a little to stir things up.

Eighth Level of Existence: Experientialistic

Eighth-level individuals communicate with external force via meditation. Their relationships with the outside force resemble a partnership rather than a superior-subordinate relationship. Man at this level operates on a seemingly universal theory about the destiny of man. These people usually reflect a highly intuitive genius. Graves (1970) stated:

> Since eighth level man need not attend to the problems of his existence (for him they have been solved) he values those

> newer, deeper things in life which are there to be experienced. He values escaping "from the barbed wire entanglement of his own ideas and his own mechanical devices." He values the "marvelous rich world of context and sheer fluid beauty and face-to-face awareness of now-naked-life." (p. 155)

Eighth-level individuals are very rare, and it is unlikely that they exist in the typical business or industry. If one should be found in business, an acceptance style of management should be used.

Conclusion

Most employers will be very familiar with Theory X and Theory Y types of administration. Few employers know the history of theories X and Y, and even fewer have ever heard of Graves. At the very least this chapter has provided some content that can give a vocational rehabilitation person something to relate to and talk about with an employer. We hope that this chapter will do more than supply vocational rehabilitation personnel with topics for discussion. We would like rehabilitation counselors to apply Graves's theory to clients and employers by determining levels of psychological existence and subsequently matching compatible relationships. Take clients at levels 3, 4, or 5 and place them with level-5 employers. Take level-6 clients and place them in a level-6 organization with level-7 management. Never place a level-4 or level-5 client under a level-6 manager or a level-3 client in a level-6 organization. Graves's theory can be of assistance to vocational rehabilitation personnel in training clients as well as recommending specific vocational treatments.

We feel that any individual who is psychologically perceptive and sensitive to the needs or existence states of others has the potential to facilitate human growth. Rehabilitation counselors are interested in assisting handicapped individuals with suitable vocational placement. However, securing and holding a job is only one side of the rehabilitation coin. The other deals with clients' feelings of contentment and happiness about themselves, not only as workers but as people. A warning must go to the counselor who is predominantly functioning in the level-6 area. Level-6 counselors have a difficult time understanding lower-level clients and employers. Level-6 counselors must remember that they are in the minority and, for the majority of people, growth is best accomplished through authoritative management practices. We hope someday (soon) the majority of people will develop to the sixth level and above so that Theory Y management, with its assumptions about man, will be a viable, feasible, and beneficial system of management for the masses.

References

Cook, D. L. The Hawthorne effect in educational research. *Phi Delta Kappan,* 1962, *44,* 116–122.

Festinger, L., & Katz, D. (Eds.) *Research methods in the behavioral sciences.* New York: Dryden Press, 1953.

Graves, C. W. The deterioration of work standards. *Harvard Business Review,* 1966, *44,* 117–126.

Graves, C. W. Levels of existence: An open system theory of values. *Journal of Humanistic Psychology,* 1970, *10,* 131–155.

Knezevich, S. J. *Administration of public education.* New York: Harper & Brothers, 1962.

Likert, R. *The human organization: Its management and value.* New York: McGraw-Hill, 1967.

Management Center Staff, Institute for Business and Community Development, University of Richmond. Clare W. Graves' theory of levels of human existence and suggested managerial systems for each level. Unpublished manuscript, 1971.

McGregor, D. *The human side of enterprise.* New York: McGraw-Hill, 1960.

Myers, M. S., & Myers, S. S. Adapting to the new work ethic. *Business Quarterly,* 1973, *38*(4), 48–58.

Roethlisberger, F. J., & Dickson, W. J. *Management and the worker.* Cambridge, Mass.: Harvard University Press, 1939.

Schein, E. H. *Organizational psychology.* (2nd ed.) Englewood Cliffs, N.J.: Prentice-Hall, 1970.

Taylor, F. W. *The principles of scientific management.* New York: Harper & Brothers, 1913.

Townsend, R. *Up the organization.* New York: Alfred A. Knopf, 1970.

Part II

VOCATIONAL ADJUSTMENT OF THE HANDICAPPED

Chapter 5

APPROACHING EMPLOYERS

Throughout the history of the state-federal program of vocational rehabilitation in America, one of the most important aspects of the rehabilitation process has been vocational placement. In more recent years, economic conditions have made this phase even more difficult to achieve, and therefore many agencies have been motivated to create job classifications for "placement specialists," or some similar title. If one discusses the responsibilities of such a position with placement specialists, however, one soon learns that they usually have very little (if any) specialized training in placement, they usually function within poorly defined limits, and they are often not held in the highest esteem by their colleagues in casework management. Placement specialists may be employees of the local school system or the state Division of Vocational Rehabilitation or possibly both, but regardless of where the salary comes from the task to be done is simple and straightforward; that is, to place clients in jobs.

Once the client is ready for either temporary (more training necessary) or permanent placement in a job, employers have to be contacted before placements can be made. Since some information about community employers will already be available to the placement person, the question now is, where do we go from here? Does the rehabilitation counselor simply contact several employers and ask them to place a client? The answer is a qualified no. Before employers are contacted, the rehabilitation counselor or placement person should consider the type of participation sought from a certain employer. In this regard, an employer can become involved in a vocational preparation program in at least five different ways. An employer can (1) provide the worker with a job, (2) provide training for the worker, (3) advise program personnel concerning technical aspects of the program, (4) aid in securing other employers to work with the program, and (5) assist in public relations efforts. In many instances, the first two roles are the most desirable. However, when an employer assumes any of the last three roles, it does allow other program personnel to be released from these tasks.

Since the first two roles of the employer are of greatest concern to the rehabilitation counselor, our attention now moves to developing an approach for effective and efficient placement of students on jobs. Most rehabilitation counselors who have had any success in the placement process will readily admit that their approach is largely the result of innumerable trial-and-error experiences, and this is a tragic state of affairs in a human service delivery system. In fact, after counselors or placement specialists have worked in placement for a year or two, they may be considered lucky if they have developed *one* good sales approach. By way of contrast, professional salespeople are taught their profession in three distinct stages. First, they are given all the *information* available regarding their product, be it encyclopedias, insurance, waterless cookware, or vacuum cleaners. Second, they are taught what is thought to be the most effective method of *presenting* the product to the potential buyer. Third, they are taught how to *sell* the product to the consumer; that is, how to overcome "I can't afford it" and "I don't need it." Most placement specialists would be hard pressed to cite similar experiences in their preparation and/or training backgrounds. Rehabilitation counselors have a need for an approach similar to that of salespeople in order to overcome employer objections and make the placement process more efficient. This chapter offers one such approach, which involves three types of employers and a three-phase method for approaching these employers differentially.

Approaching Different Types of Employers

As mentioned in Section I, Dr. Clare W. Graves of Union College in Schenectady, New York, has devoted approximately 20 years to the development of his open system theory of values (Graves, 1970), often referred to as Graves's psychological levels of existence (Payne, Mercer, & Epstein, 1974). The theory holds that all people develop through a series of psychological levels in which their needs, value systems, and motivators differ, and hence they respond differently to their environments. The descriptions of the levels include enough basic information so that people may be identified at specific stages in their developmental processes. Additionally, ideas and suggestions emerge as to how to deal with individuals differently. As a result, we have come to refer to the utilization of this system as *differential management,* and we believe that a more systematic approach can be learned and used for effective and efficient placement by applying the theoretical model to the rehabilitation placement process. We have found that most employers may be grouped in three categories: (1) conformist, (2) materialistic, and (3) sociocentric.

Conformist employers

Conformists are most often conservative employers, usually those who are operating their own proprietorships. They have generally pulled themselves up by their own bootstraps, and they believe that the way to get ahead is through perseverance, keeping one's shoulder to the wheel and nose to the grindstone. Often employers of this type are family people and have started and developed their businesses primarily for their family. They devoutly believe in the worth of rules and regulations, and they usually run their organizations in an autocratic fashion, with many policies and guidelines to be followed—sometimes posted for the employees to see. Their organizations may be described as rigid, and this characterization is often exemplified by the presence of a time clock on which *everybody* punches in and out. Conformist employers view themselves as pillars of the community. They believe they have a responsibility to civic organizations and just causes, but they should not be viewed as easy marks by placement personnel, because they sometimes believe that handicapped individuals are being punished by some powerful outside source and therefore they will not be too sympathetic.

Materialistic employers

Materialistic employers are more cause-and-effect oriented. They are "slicker"; that is, rather than persevering to get ahead, they are seen as more calculating or manipulative. They believe that it's who you know rather than what you know that counts. They are production oriented, making extensive use of charts and graphs, and are usually very successful. They like to display their success through the purchase of digital watches and portable calculators, by driving large, flashy cars, and by dressing in the latest fashion. On the whole, they look and act just as a sharp business person would be expected to look and act.

Sociocentric employers

Sociocentric employers are a relatively new breed who have come to the forefront only within the last decade. While these individuals are rare, they are quite important. They have usually inherited their businesses from their fathers or close relatives. Employers fitting this category are not production oriented but rather people oriented, believing that the real purpose in life is not to make money or develop a large corporation. They feel that the real life purpose of the individual is to get along with people, to love, to develop friendship. Thus, many sociocentric employers are opposed to competition and often just want to get the job done. These employers build their organizations around employees, and their businesses often take on a "one big, happy family" atmosphere. As a matter of fact, the success of the sociocentric employer's organization is often judged by how well his or her employees get along among themselves.

One seldom has difficulty getting in to see sociocentric employers because the door is always open. They may appear at first glance to be easy to sell the placement program to, but one should not be deceived. Many of these employers are really difficult to sell ideas to because they do not like to make unilateral decisions. Committee actions rather than those taken by autocratic processes characterize the daily operations of businesses led by sociocentric employers.

A Three-Phase Approach

Since these three categories of employers differ significantly, we have developed three distinct approaches to placing a handicapped individual in their organizations. The approaches all follow a three-phase plan consisting of (1) acquisition, (2) development, and (3) maintenance. Acquisition refers to the initial approach or contact (getting one's foot in the door to present a program; development refers to actually getting the employer to place a handicapped person on the job; and maintenance refers to the actual hiring of a handicapped person on a paid, full-time basis. Each of these phases will be described for each category of employer.

Acquisition

As with any introductory relationship, the first order of business is that which has become known as the establishment of rapport. This phrase probably strikes a harmonic chord with most readers because its extensive use spans courses in counseling, special education, psychological testing, and other related fields. Unfortunately, few professors explain *how* to establish rapport. They often assume everyone knows how to establish rapport just as everyone knows how to shake hands. Those who experience the "wet fish" handshake have grown to doubt the innateness of this skill, and we believe that the process of establishing rapport must also be learned. Therefore, one of the primary goals in this chapter will be to present useful information about how to establish rapport.

Initially, many people are at a loss for words and/or ideas for talking with others. Therefore, the presentation of useful tips on establishing rapport with each type of employer is an important goal at this point.

Conformist employers. Conformist employers dress in a conservative fashion, and they usually look uncomfortable when attired semiformally; for example, when they wear sports coats and ties. They wear plain brown or black shoes that are usually a little scuffed, and a preference for white socks is not uncommon among them. Their offices have a Rotary Club sign or other civic organization plaque displayed on the wall, generally indicating years of service rendered. An association with an organization over a period of time is important to these individuals. Family pictures are usually displayed on their desks and, of course, casual conversation regarding families can be initiated, since conformist employers, like most of us, enjoy talking about their families. When placement specialists also share pictures and/or anecdotes about their own families, a common ground has been achieved and rapport is being established. If the specialist does not have a family, conversation about the armed services, church activities, local politics, Rotary clubs or CB radios is often successful.

Once rapport has been established, the rehabilitation counselor may begin to present his program or product. It is best to remember that the conformist employer is a traditionalist who will best respond to a presentation of dedication and sincerity. The approach should be brief, direct, and matter-of-fact. If possible, it is most helpful to furnish the employer with a formal printed outline of the prepared presentation. Along with the outline, it may be helpful to offer a pencil imprinted with the placement specialist's name and telephone number in the event that the employer wishes to take notes. Do not deviate from the prepared outline, and on leaving present the conformist with a traditional black-on-white business card. Be certain that gratitude is expressed for the person's investment of time.

Materialistic employers. Materialistic employers are recognized with relative ease, since they demonstrate their success by wearing their accomplishments "on the cuff," so to speak. Their manner of dress is quite fashionable, and we have found that almost all of them seem to enjoy talking about shoes. As strange as this may sound, most of them wear well-shined expensive shoes (Florsheim wing tips are a favorite) in a proud display of their footwear. While these actions appear to be unconsciously motivated, only slight encouragement is needed to elicit a short dissertation on the construction, history, and of course the cost of these and other possessions.

The offices of materialistic employers are more plush than those of the conformist, with elaborate floor coverings that have been personally selected. Civic club plaques and membership certificates will be proudly displayed and will most often indicate positions held in the organization rather than years of service. If group family portraits are displayed in the materialistic employer's office, they will be nicely matted and framed. Under no circumstances will those individuals have snapshots casually placed on a desk or credenza. Unlike the conformist, materialistic employers do not necessarily want to discuss their families since such matters are virtually dissociated from business and the attainment of success. They may, however, desire to expound on their children's accomplishments in school, local organizations, and athletic events.

Sports are a topic that will almost certainly evoke some response in the materialistic employer and hints regarding the preferred sport can usually be obtained through surveying the office for trinkets and trophies. If the decision is made not to talk about any of the suggested topics, conversation about the furnishings of the office, latest fashion trends, or current fads that have appeal for materialistic employers may prove successful. Among the latter are pinky rings, putters, graphite-shaft drivers, and the newest of the power-designed steel tennis rackets.

Once rapport has been established, be aware that these individuals respect and admire competence and will expect a polished approach that is not regimented. Materialistic employers want to be convinced that they should participate in the rehabilitation process and are attracted by novel approaches and by such slogans as "It pays to hire the handicapped." Be prepared, however, to substantiate any such claim with facts and figures. It may be decided to use visual aids (charts, graphs, pictures, dossiers, etc.) when possible. Materialistic employers are realistic and want to be presented with the weaknesses as well as the strengths of the placement prospect. This means that they want to know exactly what the client can and cannot do. Caution must be exercised in using diagnostic labels or other technical terms, since these people often become confused by them.

Having made the presentation in as brief and comprehensive a fashion as possible, present the materialistic employer with an expensive-looking business card, preferably one that is embossed or engraved. These people respond positively to boldness, so do not hesitate to use an off-beat color like chartreuse or fiery red.

Sociocentric employers. Sociocentric employers tend to be more casual in all respects than either of the other categories. In terms of dress, they prefer sweaters, sports shirts, and comfortable footwear. (Hush Puppies are a favorite, but in extreme cases one may encounter Earth shoes, sandals, or thongs.) If a person is encountered in a hiring situation who isn't wearing socks, you are almost certainly confronting a sociocentric employer.

Sociocentric employers maintain informal offices that are often decorated with posters proclaiming that "Today is the first day of the rest of your life," or those stating the Gestalt Prayer. Comments about these posters, pictures taped or pinned to the wall, and other office adornments will be favorably received. Ecology, alternate forms of energy, sailing, backpacking, bicycling, zero population growth, and topics of a similar nature are always of interest to the sociocentric individual. Rehabilitation counselors should focus more on the employer's organizations than on their own. Interest should be shown in matters that are of concern to sociocentrics, and their primary concerns are, of course, in the affective realm of people, feelings, fellowship, togetherness.

Since sociocentric employers do not like to make decisions alone, the placement specialist must be perceived as real, trustworthy, and sincere before the sociocentric employer will entertain the idea of trying a client. Therefore, it is most important that sales pressure *not* be applied too quickly, if ever!

When departing from the sociocentric employer's office for the first time, instead of leaving a business card, pull from your purse or jacket a small piece of paper (preferably recycled paper), maybe one that says at the top "From the desk of . . . ." On it you should write (or preferably print) your address and telephone number with a bold marking pencil. This personal touch, this act of spontaneity, will have great appeal.

It must have become clear by now that a good placement program person must be almost incredibly multifaceted to establish rapport. Moreover, once rapport has been established and the vocational program presented, only the acquisition phase has been accomplished. After the employer has agreed to try a handicapped person on a job, the development phase has begun.

Development

During the development phase, the rehabilitation counselor's effort will be toward assisting the employer in developing confidence in working with handicapped individuals. It is crucial that employers do not feel that they have hastily acquired a handicapped worker. The placement person's role should be a supportive one, constantly reassuring employers that they aren't alone in the rehabilitation process.

The techniques involved in the development phase, while simple to master, are rather difficult to implement because of the time required for continued contact. The placement person must view the development phase a a partnership with the employer. Many programs have excellent procedures but fail to provide the supportive services necessary to assure ongoing employer involvement.

Conformist employers merely need to be told and retold

how important they are to the rehabilitation process. It is necessary to explain to these employers that without their interest and support there would be no rehabilitation process. Conformists must be constantly reminded of this and appreciated for their involvement. In times of stress and conflict, the placement person will be expected to stand in support of both the client and the employer. Solutions to problems are expected to be direct and should usually be presented in "cookbook" fashion.

Materialistic employers want to be shown how important they are rather than being told. They are not interested in comparing handicapped employees with so-called "normal" employees. They do, however, want to see signs of improvement and growth. Moreover, this improvement and growth does not have to be demonstrated through production; rather, it can be shown by data that document improved attendance, numbers of positive comments toward the job, changes in appearance, and so on. Rehabilitation counselors must develop skills and a sensitivity for finding important working variables and behaviors, and they must devise ways of observing and measuring these variables in small increments so that improvement and growth can be shown.

Since sociocentric employers are neither competitive nor production minded, they must discover that the placement situation is working. Their major concern will be whether or not the handicapped individual fits into their family-type organizational structure. During the development phase, the rehabilitation counselor should ask leading questions that are designed to engage the employer in talking about the client. When problems arise, sociocentrics want to be involved rather than being told or shown how important they are. This involvement is encouraged by a type of questioning that turns problems back to the employer for potential solutions. Gradually, they discover that they are very important because they are solving the problems without anyone telling them what to do and how to do it.

Maintenance

Finally, the maintenance phase is achieved when the employer is ready to assume the client as a full-time, independent employee. The maintenance process for all three categories of employers is the same; that is, employers don't really need the placement person as much as they previously did because they have reached a state of knowing they are good.

Conformist employers no longer need to be told that they are important. As a matter of fact, they usually go around giving testimonials and become advocates of hiring the handicapped. Materialistic employers share with other employers documents that indicate success, and they will often apply to other employees the same techniques they have used with the handicapped. Sociocentric employers intuitively arrive at the decision that all is going well, and they may request that other handicapped clients be sent for employment in the future.

A word of caution is necessary here, for just as sociocentric employers avoid making decisions about hiring handicapped people, it is often difficult for them to stop hiring them. In this event, sociocentrics may push their businesses ever closer to bankruptcy through their hiring practices alone, since they often employ the most limited and difficult-to-place individuals in rehabilitation case loads. After the sociocentric employer has attained maintenance skills, protection may become an important part of the placement person's role by restricting the future placement of handicapped individuals with that organization.

Summary of Three-Phase Approach

Table 5-1 summarizes the essential information for approaching three types of employers following a three-phase approach consisting of acquisition, development, and maintenance. The summary table contains three types of employers with three separate phases for each, forming a three-by-three matrix, making a total of nine cells or blocks. Each of the three employers has an acquisition cell, a development cell, and a maintenance cell. These cells contain a summary of the main ideas and hints as to how the placement specialist should approach each of the three employers.

For instance, each acquisition cell contains topics for discussion to establish rapport, followed by suggestions that will enhance the presentation. For example, for the conformist em-

Table 5-1.
Summary of Three-Phase Approach

	Conformist Employers	*Materialistic Employers*	*Sociocentric Employers*
Acquisition	Civic Club Plaques (years of service) Family Pictures Armed Services Church Activities Local Politics ---------- Outline of Presentation Black-on-White Business Cards	Civic Club Plaques (position held) Children's Accomplishments Florsheim Wing-tip Shoes Fads and Fashions Sports ---------- Impressive Presentation (graphs, charts, visual aids, etc.) Expensive-looking Business Cards	Ecology Alternate Forms of Energy Sailing Backpacking Bicycling Zero Population Growth ---------- Nonpressured, Sincere Presentation Personal Note on Recycled Paper
Development	Support Told and Retold Constantly Reminded of Importance	Show Demonstrate Progress Graphs or Charts on Attendance, Production, Appearance, etc.	Discover Ask Leading Question Involve in Problem Solving
Maintenance			

ployer an outline of the presentation and a black-on-white business card are important; the materialistic employer wants to be sold, so graphs and charts are recommended along with an expensive business card; finally, the sociocentric employer needs a nonpressured approach to instill trust, along with a personal note on recycled paper rather than a business card. The development cells for the three employers offer suggestions on how to keep the employer involved in the program or rehabilitation process. For example, conformist employers need to be acknowledged and reminded of how important they are to the program or rehabilitation process; materialistic employers need to be shown that the client is progressing; and sociocentric employers need to be involved in the program by taking an active part in solving problems related to the clients they employ. The acquisition and development cells contain information on approaching the three employers differentially. The maintenance phase for the three employers is the same, with all three cells left blank to indicate that the employer does not need the placement person as much as before. Ideally, employers who have reached the maintenance phase have become skilled and confident enough to employ clients effectively, thereby allowing the intense involvement of the placement person in the acquisition and developmental phases. Once an employer is in the maintenance phase, the placement person should have more time to place other clients, starting with acquisition and going through the three-phase process again.

Conclusion

The placement process is complex, and there are specific skills and techniques that can be learned to aid the vocational placement of handicapped clients. It is important for rehabilitation counselors to possess a vast amount of knowledge about specific jobs, to thoroughly understand their products, and to cultivate skills and techniques regarding the presentation and sale of their products. It is also necessary for rehabilitation counselors and placement specialists to know a great deal about the needs of employers, how to establish rapport with them, and how to carry out a detailed placement plan from acquisition to development to maintenance. The next chapter further explains how to develop and maintain employer support.

References

Graves, C. W. Levels of existence: An open system theory of values. *Journal of Humanistic Psychology,* 1970, *10*(2), pp. 131–155.

Payne, J. S., Mercer, D. C., & Epstein, M. H. *Education and rehabilitation techniques.* New York: Behavioral Publications, Inc., 1974.

Chapter 6.

DEVELOPING AND MAINTAINING EMPLOYER SUPPORT

After rapport has been established and the employer has at least agreed to give a handicapped individual a chance to work, efforts should then be directed toward further developing the employer's interest in working with handicapped individuals as well as increasing the employer's skills in training and managing.

When a counselor's case load includes a handicapped client who, after completing some type of training routine, *is employable*, everything is satisfactory, and the client, counselor, and employer are happy. Unfortunately, most vocational training programs do not go according to game plan; that is, most handicapped workers experience difficulty in securing and holding jobs. If handicapped workers had little or no difficulty in employment endeavors, there would be little need for comprehensive vocational rehabilitation programs.

Articles printed in weekly and monthly magazines, advertisements over radio and television, and billboard signs along the highways report the vocational rehabilitation client as a non-handicapped individual. Employers are told by the government and news media that the handicapped want to make good; will work particularly hard to make good; are not anxious to change jobs frequently; are happy to learn a job and remain with it; have an attendance record that is usually better than average; will stay with routine tasks; come to work dependably and on time; are quiet, well behaved, and inclined not to gossip or "goof off"; are well trained vocationally; take pride in their work and try hard to please; and do not get restless.

In some cases guarantees are made to the employer. The prospective employer can be certain the client is not a misfit; is a competent worker; is stable and takes pride in his work; has a high degree of loyalty, enthusiasm, and dependability; and, above all, can perform his job well.

All of the above statements have been taken from various rehabilitation advertisements. Today's watchword is "It pays to hire the handicapped." To put it mildly, the rehabilitation client is probably being slightly oversold. The nice, easygoing, well-rounded, eager, punctual, trustworthy, loyal, helpful, friendly, courteous, kind, obedient, cheerful, thrifty, brave, and clean individual is a Boy Scout, not a vocational rehabilitation client.

Many handicapped clients make good workers, but few if any are "as advertised." In most cases even the good workers are developed after some type of training, and after the training (no matter how good and thorough it is) handicapped clients need a period of time to *adjust to the job* even if they have acquired the necessary job skills.

The ultimate success of job adjustment and rehabilitation rests with an interested employer. The successful placement of handicapped workers is not a job that can be done by well-wishers or do-gooders, or through the use of snappy slogans. It is a job that requires professional skills and knowledge, and it must be done on an individual basis. The capabilities and limitations of the individual client must be realized. Also, the employer's needs must be gauged by visiting the place of employment and noting the job skill requirements, the kinds of people employed, and the working climate (Pinner, 1960). Counselors must develop and perfect skills for enhancing employer interest in working with the handicapped.

DEVELOPING EMPLOYER INTEREST

An employer's interest may be enhanced in a number of ways. One technique is to "lead with a winner." Providing a fairly good worker as the employer's first trainee will reduce any anxiety the employer may have developed about participating in the program. There is almost universal agreement that, in opening up work samples, work sites, or job placement situations, it is always best to begin with a client who is most likely to succeed. This appears feasible until a counselor realizes that his case load no longer includes "good ones". In the Kansas Work Study Program it was demonstrated that it is possible to lead off with high-risk clients and still maintain employer interest. For example, clients were placed in a local cafeteria on four occasions, and all four times they did a miserable job. However, the clients were able to learn and profit from their experiences, and the cafeteria's personnel and facilities served valuable training purposes. In addition, on the average of once every 2 months the counselor received a call from the personnel manager asking if anyone else could be placed there. It was not known if they were trying to prepare for another client or if they actually wanted some more clients (Payne, 1966). Nevertheless, the door was always open. The reason it was possible to lead off with poor workers and still keep the employers participating was that the program and not the client was sold via honest and accurate communication.

Another way to increase the employer's interest in working with the handicapped is to emphasize constantly the importance of his or her role in the program. The best way for a client to learn to work is actually to work. This assumption makes the employer the central figure in the training program. Straightforward and unsophisticated statements, such as "If it weren't for your assistance, John might never have learned to work," can be very meaningful and effective in developing the employer's interest. The staightforward yet sincere approach is invaluable to employers at the conformist level and the sociocentric level. Conformist employers want to be told directly and specifically how important they are. Sociocentric employers want to feel they are important because others like them. They do not want to be viewed as manipulators. Therefore, a positive comment might be a statement such as "If it weren't for your concern and sincere interest in John, he might never have come as far as he has." Materialistic employers like to be told and shown how important they are as is illustrated next.

A third method for increasing employers' interest is to reinforce their participation by reporting changes observed in the handicapped employee during his tenure with the employer. Changes in behavior almost always occur when a client is placed on a new job, and they should be communicated to the employer, especially if the employer is functioning within the materialistic level. The alert counselor is aware of these changes and reports them to the employer through the use of such statements as "You sure shaped up John's appearance since he started with you," or "John averaged five tardies a week before he started on this job. Now he is late only about twice a week." Showing the employer specific changes in a client's work behavior is most impressive and appreciated by any employer but especially by the materialistic employer. The materialistic employer likes to see cause and effect and believes he can make things happen. Manipulation is a way of life to materialistic employers, and they view it as a positive means of helping handicapped workers learn and adjust to their job. Conformist employers like to see changes but do not necessarily need to be shown they were the cause of the change. Sociocentric employers like to see change in clients but only if the clients verbalize that they like the work, their job, their employer, and so on. Showing the sociocentric employer changes in the client always should be accompanied with statements such as "He's smiling more," or "She doesn't have that chip on her shoulder any more," or "He was telling me the other day that he is the happiest he has ever been in a long, long time."

All of these techniques may be used to develop the interest of the employer in working with handicapped clients. A different approach is required when the objective is to assist the employer in improving his training techniques when working with vocational rehabilitation clients.

Developing Employer Training Skills

An effective means of teaching employers techniques for training handicapped clients is behavioral management. Behavioral management skills do not have to be taught in a classroom or laboratory setting but rather on a casual or informal basis. The first step in helping employers to develop behavior-management skills is to persuade them to describe the client's work behavior in precise, descriptive, behavioral terms rather than with intuitive or general impressions. This approach is based on the rationale that knowing that a client is "not getting along well" or "seems unhappy" does not provide useful information for a corrective training program. If the employer is to report precise and descriptive information, it is necessary for him or her to observe behavior in an objective manner. If the employer feels that a youngster is "not doing well," he or she should attempt to specify the behaviors that give that impression. It may be that the client "works slowly," "fumbles with materials," or "spends a lot of time in the rest room." This kind of information, while still somewhat imprecise, can provide some basis for a corrective program.

Employers should be encouraged to carry a small notebook and record specific behaviors for later reference. The skillfull counselor often can prompt employers to count and record the frequency of some behaviors that he feels are important. Knowledge of the frequency of occurrences, both before and after the application of corrective techniques, adds considerable precision to the training program and leads into the actual teaching of behavior-management techniques. Conformist and materialist employers can and will record behaviors, but sociocentric employers would totally refuse behavior-management techniques, as it would be considered too structured and confining.

The basics of teaching of behavior-management techniques to employers include: (a) identifying the problem behaviors in observable terms; (b) counting the frequency of problem behaviors; (c) doing something about it (treat, counsel, teach, train, etc.); and (d) determining if the treatment improved the situation by counting the frequency of problem behaviors during and after treatment. If enough change has not been found, another treatment or treatments should be tried.

The following situation illustrates the behavior-management technique. An employer says that a client is doing poorly on the job because he is not motivated. Since motivation cannot be observed, it is necessary to determine what not being motivated is in observable and possibly quantifiable terms. Through further questioning it is found that the client is projecting nonmotivation by arriving late to work. The employer reveals the client's time card and it is discovered he is late for work 2 or 3 days a week. The vocational treatment might be to talk with the client about the problem. The employer checks the time card the following week to determine the effectiveness of the treatment. If appropriate changes have been made, success has been experienced with this aspect of job motivation. However, if no success is experienced, other types of treatment will have to be tried.

Typical vocational cases report tardiness due to a number of factors, including (a) client not being able to tell time, (b) no alarm clock, (c) lack of knowledge about how to set the alarm clock, (d) transportation difficulties, (e) not understanding the importance of arriving at work on time, and (f) lack of enough sleep the previous night. Regardless of the numerous reasons for the client's tardiness, the use of the behavior-management schema at least determines the behavioral problems and facilitates the development of appropriate intervention strategies.

In general, for all three types of employers, during the developmental phase it is extremely important for the counselor to visit at regular intervals. Contacts should be made at least once a week. Also, the counselor should respond immediately if the employer requests help. A phrase often used is "I'm as close as the telephone." Employer visits can consume a considerable amount of staff time, but as employers become better trainers they can work more independently. Careful execution of the developmental phase is essential to success in the final phase of maintaining the employer's support.

Maintaining Employer Support

During the previous phase the counselor served as a reinforcer for the employer through statements concerning the client that made the employer feel that what he was doing was successful and worthwhile. The controlling factor in the maintenance phase is the *employer's ability to recognize changes in the client without being told or prompted by the counselor.* This can be brought about by having the counselor phrase questions that will elicit verbal responses from the employer concerning changes in the client's behavior. Once elicited, these responses can be reinforced. The initial stages of this phase will require direct contact by the counselor with the employer. However, visits can be less frequent and less regular than during the development phase.

The key to maintaining employer support is to facilitate the development of interest and skills in employers so that they can determine what the problem is, how severe the problem is (record and quantify the problem behaviors), and what to do about it. Employer conferences represent a training device used by counselors to assist employers in the development and maintenance of training skills.

Employer Conference

The employer conference is a monthly meeting attended by employers, supervisors, and vocational personnel who are responsible for the vocational adjustment of handicapped clients. It is best to limit the conference to 10 employers and/or supervisors at a given time. These management representatives act as consultants, and the conferences are designed to provide opportunities to discuss specific problems related to hiring the handicapped. Employer conferences complement any vocational program and are important in the development and maintenance of interest and skills related to working with handicapped clients. The conference, however, should not be considered a replacement for individual contact and supervision by the vocational counselor. Employer conferences contribute to the success of a training program in many ways, such as improved client placement, more adequate supervision of clients, employer identification with the project, acquisition of new work sites, teaching and training implications, aids to employer understanding of workers in general, improved communication, and improved client evaluation.

Improved Client Placement

As a client's work experience is discussed, it is not unusual for an employer to suggest a particular job in his establishment that might be suitable for certain clients with specific limitations. For example, at one employer conference two former employers of a trainee concluded that the client could benefit from a routine job that would allow him to work side by side and in cooperation with another person (this client had a lot of level-2 characteristics). Another employer replied, "If that's the case, I'd like to try him on one of my folding machines, with the job of folding sheets. All he would have to do is take out the sheets and fold them with the help of another person. I can regulate the machine to run as fast or slow as I want. This should be just the thing he needs."

How to train and where to place the more limited clients is a serious problem in most vocational programs. As programs get started, the number of work sites is limited; therefore, the more restricted clients are very difficult to place. During employer conferences it is advisable to discuss specific clients and their limitations. Usually an employer will volunteer to attempt to work with a very limited client on a specific job. Some employers will adjust the duties and tasks of a job to fit the client's abilities. No one knows more about particular jobs than employers, and it is interesting to see how employers communicate among themselves and how they are able to adapt the tasks to fit an individual client. One specific example of this occurred in a high-volume restaurant in which the employer trained an extremely limited youngster as a garnish person. Usually a garnish person is required to move very fast, possess much finger dexterity, and be able to think fast in order to get the correct garnish on the right sandwiches. This employer divided the garnishing job into small steps. First, as the sandwiches crossed in front of the handicapped employee, he was required only to place two pickles on each sandwich. After doing this for approximately 2 weeks, the client was instructed to place the two pickles on the sandwich and then add mustard. Next the client was instructed to differentiate between sandwiches that needed pickles and mustard from sandwiches that needed mayonnaise, lettuce, and tomato. (Another employee had been garnishing the mayonnaise, lettuce, and tomato sandwiches while the handicapped client was learning the pickle-and-mustard operation. Thus, during the initial weeks of the training program, the handicapped client saw and garnished only those sandwiches that needed mustard and pickle.) Over a period of time the client was able to function adequately in this job. To give an idea of the number of sandwiches handled by the client, this restaurant would use over 18 dozen buns within less than an hour, a pace representing over 200 sandwiches per hour for a 3-hour period. When the client worked on the sample, he handled over 650 sandwiches during the lunch period.

More Adequate Supervision of Clients

Since the conference occurs at a convenient time, when the employers are not distracted by daily routine, the vocational staff may easily acquire and disseminate information about a specific client as well as the project in general. Also, it cannot be overlooked that some employers learn from fellow employers. An example of this occurred when one employer mentioned how a client manipulated the employer into doing some of the client's work. She explained that when the client would slow down to an extremely low production level on tasks she disliked, the employer ended up helping or sending another employee to assist the client. On a couple of occasions the employer ended up doing the work while the client stood and watched. On hearing this, another employer smiled and interrupted the conversation to explain how he had been manipulated into transporting a client home. During the winter months the employer drove the client to the bus stop so that the client would not have to walk in the bad weather. However, when the weather was pleasant, the employer still found himself transporting the client to the bus stop. When the employer refused to drive the client to the bus stop during good weather conditions, the client began staying overtime, which caused him to miss his bus. Thus, the employer was placed in the situation of transporting the client *all the way home.* Needless to say, after the employer's conference both of these situations were solved by the respective employers.

Employer Identification with the Project

It is important for the conformist employer initially to feel that he or she is an integral part of the rehabilitation team. The employer conference is an excellent means for projecting this. Also, thank-you letters from staff and clients help to express the importance of the employer. Allowing employers an opportunity to share experiences informally promotes employer identification with the rehabilitation process. This is especially true with sociocentric employers who like to share and experience knowledge.

Acquisition of New Work Sites

As an active member of his community, the employer has frequent associations with other employers in both social and professional realms. It is not uncommon for participating employers to invite other employers to attend the employer conferences. As the vocational program is discussed, the new employers frequently offer work samples and placement sites. For instance, most conformist employers are members of a variety of civic organizations, and they often invite another vocational staff member to share information about the vocational program. Presentations of this type are excellent for enlisting the participation of new employers.

Teaching and Training Implications

Employer conferences are an excellent source for obtaining ideas about teaching job-related activities and skills. On one occasion a client was working at a high-volume ice cream parlor, and it was discovered that she was experiencing difficulty in making correct change. Previously the client had gone through a comprehensive change-making instructional unit. Even though the client had successfully completed the unit, she still made mistakes on the job. As the problem was discussed among the employers, one employer suggested that, since the mistakes were always under five cents, perhaps she could not read the tax chart. Upon further investigation it was discovered that the client was confused about the proper procedure for using the tax chart. Many different types of tax charts were secured and a tax chart subunit was added to the change-making instructional unit.

Aids to Employer Understanding of Workers in General

Employers frequently mention that what they learn at the employer conferences is directly applicable to other employees. Careful observation and simple methods of treatment, as exemplified in the behavior management approach, are essential to good training and evaluation for all workers. In other words, employers are discovering that the methods that work for handicapped clients are excellent techniques to use with all employees.

Improved Communication

Improved communication between vocational staff and employers is probably the most important aspect of the employer conference. Terminology used by the professional rehabilitation staff is not always understood by participating employers. An example of this is the manner in which employers toss around the term "initiative" as if it were understood by all concerned. Actually, initiative means different things in different businesses. To some employers, the term "self-starter" would coincide with initiative, and to others initiative means starting to work on time and working without being told. Initiative also may mean willingness to work overtime. Through the employer conference, both the employer and the vocational rehabilitation staff find common ground for communication.

Conclusion

This chapter offers several suggestions for developing and maintaining employer support. To begin with, statements regarding the advertising of handicapped workers were listed. This was followed by a discussion on developing employer interests, training, and support. Finally, the employer conference was described in detail. Specific situations were discussed in which the conference improved client placement, helped employers feel a part of the program, and offered employers an opportunity to communicate with each other about training and understanding handicapped workers.

As employers learn to observe and record specific behaviors occurring on the job, the foundation for an accurate and beneficial evaluation system has been established. Evaluation techniques are constantly under revision, and through employer conferences these techniques are refined. Because of the importance of developing effective evaluation and follow-up procedures, the next chapter will be devoted to the development of these necessary skills.

References

Payne, J. S. Kansas vocational rehabilitation and special education cooperative project. In J. D. Chaffin, L. Edwards, & F. Hudson (Eds.), *Workshop on cooperative development of vocational rehabilitation services to the handicapped in public schools.* Lawrence, Kans.: University of Kansas, 1966.

Pinner, J. I. New York State employment service's experience in placing the mentally retarded. In The Woods Schools, *Outlook for the adult retarded.* Langhorne, Pa.: The Woods Schools, 1960.

Chapter 7.

EVALUATION AND FOLLOW-UP

An important facet of any vocational program is obtaining information about the client in a job situation. At the present time many vocational programs use a check sheet, which in some cases is given to the employer or direct supervisor to complete. This type of evaluation sheet covers a number of general areas, which will be discussed later. However, it is of benefit to discuss first the rationale for work evaluations and their uses.

In the Minneapolis program (Project 681) it is stated that 77 of 138 terminated clients were released from their jobs because of inadequate attitudes and motivation patterns. Thirty were dismissed because of their inability to handle their job duties and instructions. Other projects have described similar reasons for job terminations, and thus the evaluation and employer feedback are vital if fewer failures are to be experienced.

In the field of rehabilitation, learning is frequently by trial and error. However, because of the communication barrier or breakdown between the placement person and the employer, it is extremely difficult to learn from the client's mistakes. Many times the employer is unable to interpret the mistakes in specific terms that can be communicated to the client. Feedback and interpretation of problems are of paramount importance and provide the rationale for evaluation sheets and follow-up sessions. Also, it should be mentioned that the knowledge gained from evaluation and follow-up sessions can be used in formal training sessions prior to placement on a community work sample. This information is invaluable to the development of a vocational curriculum. It is realized that rehabilitation has progressed throughout the years, and many excellent employer-counselor relationships have been established; however, even with these excellent relationships, it is rare for counselors to receive meaningful evaluations.

Employers usually know their jobs and people better than anyone else, but their ability to communicate specific problems and reasons for client failure on the job is usually limited. Sometimes an employer is too busy to report either orally or in written form a long detailed account concerning the success or failure of a client. Many times, if the client is a success, the employer is happy and sees little reason for an evaluation. If the client is unsuccessful, the employer sometimes has a tendency to evaluate him in general terms, such as "He lacks motivation," "He is lazy," or "He just can't cut the mustard." When a client is terminated for nonspecific reasons, it is difficult to improve the client's working ability because the specific reason for failure has not been conveyed.

How does a counselor train or counsel a client who lacks motivation or just cannot "cut the mustard"? Even though the most conscientious employer knows the client is failing, he or she often finds it difficult to express and state specific objective reasons for the client's failure.

The following example of a client working in a grocery store serves to illustrate the communication problem between counselor and employer. After 2 weeks on the job, a follow-up session with the employer revealed that the client was functioning below average. The employer diligently tried to explain why the client was failing. However, after 1 hour the only reason actually discovered was that the client was not working as fast as other employees. The reason given by the employer for this slow pace was that the client lacked motivation and was distractible. This was difficult for the placement person to believe because, during a counseling session with the client, the client frequently expressed a strong liking for the job, the employer, and so on. It was suggested that the employer carry a small piece of paper in his shirt pocket and make notes of the client's inappropriate behavior. Two days later another follow-up session occurred, and the employer's list revealed that the client reported to work on time but did not start working until 15 minutes after the starting time. Also, it mentioned that the client did not properly rotate stock, and many times he was found reading magazines. Later in the conversation with the employer it was discovered that the employer thought these were motivation factors because the client never looked busy and was not producing. When the client got off work that day, the counselor emphasized to him that people not only report to work a little before starting time but also start working on time. Also, reasons for stock rotation were explained in detail and examples were given. When the magazine problem was discussed, it was discovered that the reading of magazines on the job had nothing to do with motivation, boredom, or distractibility. In actuality, the client did not know what to do next and saw nothing wrong with looking at magazines. The counselor then explained that the client should talk to his employer about this, and if the client could not think of work to do he should consult his immediate supervisor. Needless to say, improvement was observed and reported to the counselor by the employer and much was gained by all concerned.

Many times an employer will give only one reason for a client's failure or lack of success, but probing into the situation will reveal other reasons. In fact, usually many reasons exist, expecially ones that seem small and insignificant when considered by themselves. However, when many of these small reasons are put together, an accumulation occurs and each small reason becomes quite valid.

If handicapped clients are to succeed they must perform satisfactorily. According to Scott, Dawis, England, and Lofquist (1960):

> Satisfactoriness is indicated by behavioral criteria; such as productivity, efficiency, absenteeism, disciplinary problems, etc. The literature indicates that the measurements of these criteria now available tend to fluctuate over time. Reliance on such measures taken at one point in time may be misleading. Work adjustment patterns may differ for different occupations. The set of criteria that is relevant may differ from occupation to occupation. Even if the set of relevant criteria were the same, the pattern of interrelationships among the criteria may differ. (pp. 57-58)

This is exemplified by a client who consistently reported and started to work 15 minutes prior to his regular working time. However, as a union worker, he was forced to begin work at the regular starting time.

Because job-related activities vary between and among jobs, it is difficult to teach specific tasks that will generalize to a job. Basically, there are two major problems involved in teaching work tasks or work-related activities: (a) if the tasks and/or activities are taught in general terms or at an abstract level, clients are seldom able to apply them to actual work; and (b) if a task and/or activity is specifically taught, the skill may not be transferrable to the job in which the client is placed. For instance, many clients may be taught how to mop a floor in a specific way, and they learn that specific method. However, when they go to work on a job, the clients may have to learn a new method because the particular place of business requires that it be done in a different way or with different equipment. This is paradoxical, since job skills are learned best through specific examples, but many times the specifics are not transferable to jobs. How can this problem be solved?

Possibly the best advice is to recommend that the client be taught job-related tasks and skills in a variety of situations with a variety of equipment. With this approach, the client learns that there is no *one* way to perform a task but that for each place of business there is one *accepted* way to do it. This has been referred to as *contextualistic teaching*. It is taught that in one context things are done one way and in another context another way. Rather than teaching mopping one way with one set of equipment, the skill of mopping should be taught in a variety of ways with many different kinds of equipment. By being taught in a contextualistic fashion, the client learns how to think, adapt, and solve problems.

When evaluating, it is necessary to consider the source of the evaluation. One might ask, "Why does the evaluation have to come from the employer or direct supervisor?" In some projects the entire evaluation is done by the client. In other words, the client is asked how he is doing and this information is used for the evaluation. This may be of value but, "the client whose limitations often affect his perceptions of how well or poorly he may be doing on the job also fails to enlist the aid of the counselor until after he has quit impulsively or has been dismissed." (Dubrow, 1960, p. 54) Often the client may think he or she is doing very well, but the employer reports a different story.

For example, there was a client working as a busboy in a restaurant. After 2 weeks a follow-up session with the restaurant employer was initiated. This follow-up session with the employer was initiated after a counseling session with the client, during which the client reported how well he liked the job and how well he was doing. However, during the employer follow-up session, the employer reported that the client was doing a poor job and had to be told to bus a table every time somebody got up leave the restaurant. When the employer was asked if he had discussed this directly with the client, he stated that he had and that the client was told specifically that he was not doing the job. Later in the conversation the employer revealed that he personally had told the client repeatedly to clean off certain tables. The employer had assumed that after about the two-hundredth time he had told this to his employee, the client would figure out that every time somebody got up from a table to leave the restaurant he was to bus that particular area. Needless to say, the client was unable to understand this. In fact, the client felt that he was doing a good job because the employer was paying so much attention to him.

Another similar example was that of a client in a grocery store. One task was to take a pile of potatoes and place them in small sacks so they would weigh 10 pounds each. During counseling sessions, the client expressed a strong liking for the job and his employer, and he explained that he felt he was doing a terrific job. However, during a follow-up session the employer stated that the client was working at an extremely low rate of speed. When the employer was asked if he had discussed the situation with the client directly, he assured the counselor that he had. The employer stated that he definitely told the client in such a way that he was sure the client understood. He went on to give this example: The client was sacking potatoes in the storeroom in a very slow fashion. When the employer noticed how slowly the client was working, he stepped over very close to him, placed his hands on his hips, looked the client in the eye, and said, "Boy, these potatoes are getting expensive." Then he walked away. The employer could not see how this could be interpreted any other way than that the client was doing a poor job. The client, however, thought it was good that the price of potatoes was increasing because the employer would make more money.

If the placement person had not done some probing and questioning, these important details would not have been discovered. These examples illustrate that the evaluation must come from sources other than the client. This is not to say that client self-evaluations are unimportant, but they cannot be exclusive of other evaluations. It is not practical nor feasible for the vocational counselor to observe the client directly over long periods of time and conduct the evaluation alone. This leaves the employer as an informant, and this may be the best plan because ultimately employers are the people whom the clients have to satisfy. It should be emphasized that many times the employers have the needed information, but it has been demonstrated that this information, for the most part, is difficult to obtain mainly because of a communications factor.

To enhance the communication process between the employer and the counselor, it is often necessary to use evaluation sheets. Evaluation sheets usually list of variety of factors, and the employer is asked to rate the client on a variety of work dimensions. Most checklists for evaluating handicapped clients on jobs use the following factors: (a) ability to follow directions or understand work, (b) ability to get along with co-workers as well as supervisors, (c) ability to work steadily or to sustain routine, (d) interest or motivation, (e) ability to meet production schedule or complete work on time, (f) punctuality or attendance, (g) pesonal hygiene or neatness and cleanliness, and (h) concept of self or self-confidence (see Tables 7-1, 7-2, and 7-3 for Checklist Evaluation Forms). Other factors, which are mentioned less often but may be of extreme importance, are (a) initiative, (b) safety-consciousness, (c) ability to mind own business, (d) quality of work, (e) ability to work unsupervised, (f) trustworthiness or honesty, (g) correct use of tools, (h) ability to communicate, (i) ability to perform simple counting, and (j) ability to perform simple reading. The main difficulty with the check-sheet type of evaluation seems to be that the items are too general to get a true and accurate picture of the client's performance or behavior. Also, the terms used may have an entirely different meaning to the employer than they do to vocational personnel. Another major problem with the traditional evaluation sheet is that some of the factors to be rated by the employer are factors that are taken for granted. An example of this would be the item of punctuality or reporting to work on time. It is assumed that when the employer hires the client, he or she will arrive at work on time, but there is a strong tendency to rank punctuality as a plus or bonus area on a traditional evaluation form. Actually, if the client arrives at work on time that means little to the employer because an employee is expected to be at work on time. Therefore, the only time this factor is really valid or pertinent from an evaluation standpoint is when the client fails to comply.

Regardless of what evaluation form is used, it is important to reemphasize that when the information is detailed and objective, it will be of greater value to the employer, counselor, and client. Many times "follow-up sessions are considered as a passive data gathering process; however, they need and must be viewed as an active service oriented procedure." (Dubrow, 1960, p. 55) In an enthusiastic evaluation follow-up session, it might be of value to resist the temptation of handing the employer the evaluation sheet because it might limit his responses. It is better for the placement person to have a sheet of paper divided into three

Table 7-1.
Checklist Evaluation

Client ______________________ **Date** ____________

	Excellent	*Good*	*Average*	*Not Satisfactory*
Ability to follow directions				
Ability to take correction				
Ability to sustain routine				
Ability to get along with others				
Interest in work				
Work finished on time				
Attendance				
Punctuality				
Ability to work unsupervised				
Cooperation during rush periods and overtime				
Responsibility toward company				
property and equipment				
Personal appearance				
Willingness to work steadily				
Sees things to be done				
Overall progress				

____
Employer

Table 7-2.
Checklist Evaluation

Trainee ______________________ **Date** __________

	Always	*Usually*	*Sometimes*	*Seldom*	*Never*
Understands directions					
Sustains a routine					
Accepts pressure					
Accepts criticism					
Gets along with supervisors and co-workers					
Motivated					
Works without supervision					
Observes regulations					
Apropriate appearance					
Meets production schedule					
Is a steady worker					
Does satisfactory work					
Good attention span on job					
Able to reason on job					
Trustworthy					
Uses tools correctly					
Able to express himself					
Does simple counting					
Does simple reading					

Table 7-3.
Checklist Evaluation

Trainee's Name
Employer's Name
Address
Date Started — Time on Job
Job Title — Supervisor

GROUP I
Personality and Social Adjustment

Factors	*Average Employee* Less Than	Same As	More Than	*Comments*
Self-confidence				
Cheerful				
Cooperates with supervisor				
Cooperates with other employees				
Respects supervisor				
Minds own business				
Accepts criticism				
Mixes socially with other employees				
Neat and clean				
Other				

GROUP II
Work Habits and Efficiency

Factors	*Average Employee* Less Than	Same As	More Than	*Comments*
On time				
Safety-conscious				
Careful with materials and property				

(Con't.)

Completes work on time
Quality of work
Understands work
Shows initiative
Other

Would you be as willing to hire this individual as you would your average applicant if a job were available?

Yes _____ Probably _____ Probably Not _____ No _____

If the above answer is "Probably Not" or "No," please answer the following:

Would hire IF . . . (State conditions):

columns. The headings of the three columns could be (a) positive aspects, (b) negative aspects, and (c) solution processess. When the employer discusses the client's job performance, the counselor notes the employer's comments in the proper columns. A form of this kind would be extremely simple and possibly very useful when handled by a skillful placement person (see Table 7-4 for Employer Evaluation and Training Report).

An example of reporting to work on time illustrates the use of the three-column sheet. If the person reported to work prior to his original starting time on a union job, this would be placed in the negative column, but if this were done on any other type of job, it would probably be placed in the positive column. Even though most checklists have places for comments, these comment areas are seldom used. There is a definite tendency to place check marks in the appropriate places and not write comments. With the three-column evaluation work sheet, comments must be written since there is nothing to check. With this type of evaluation form, the counselor would approach the employer with the sheet attached to a clipboard and begin the evaluation with any style of questioning that seems comfortable to the counselor-employer situation. Often a simple question such as "How is Mary doing this week?" is enough to begin discussion. As the employer

Table 7-4.
Employer Evaluation and Training Report

Trainee's Name
Job Title
Date Started
Date Completed
Employer
Name of Business
Address
Phone Number
Informant
Position

Positive Aspects	*Negative Aspects*	*Solution Processes*

talks, the counselor makes note of the salient points in the proper columns. When the employer talks in general terms such as "She can't cut the mustard," the counselor must seek clarification for specifics by questioning, "What exactly do you mean?" or "Could you give me a specific example of when and how she doesn't cut the mustard?"

Getting information down on a form of this type helps the counselor to determine quickly the client's strengths and weaknesses and provides information that can be used in a one-to-one counseling session with the client. The counselor may want the counseling session to begin with a few positive comments and end on a positive note. This procedure is simplified by selecting points of discussion from the applicable column. The three-column evaluation sheet provides a great deal of flexibility as well as an adequate amount of structure in the counseling session. Sometimes, when clients are given negative feedback, they may become overly depressed or tend to drift out of contact for awhile. By periodically injecting positive comments into the discussion, the counselor is able to keep the client involved. Positive topics for comment and discussion are readily available from the three-column evaluation sheet.

For the inexperienced counselor it may be necessary to provide more structure to the evaluation session. The counselor may have difficulty getting the employer to discuss the client. When this happens, an outline of possible evaluation factors may help the counselor to ask specific questions (see Table 7-5 for Possible

Table 7-5.
Possible Evaluation Factors

I. Individual
  A. Self-confidence (realistic)
  B. Disposition
  C. Appearance (clean, appropriate)
II. Relations with Co-workers
  A. Cooperation
  B. Attitude
  C. Interpersonal
III. Relations with Management and/or Customers
  A. Cooperation
  B. Attitude
  C. Interpersonal
  D. Criticism (effective)
IV. Vocational Expectations
  A. Attitude
  B. Distractible
  C. Punctual
  D. Careful with Property
V. Vocational Bonus Abilities
  A. Initiative (specific examples)
  B. Perseverance
  C. Production
    1. rate
    2. quality
    3. comprehension
    4. efficiency

Evaluation Factors). These evaluation factors are general and are ones often used by employers. Thus, when the employer responds to these items, the counselor may want to explore the area in more detail. For instance, the counselor might ask, "Do you feel that the client is self-confident?" Regardless of the employer's response, the counselor must ask next if this factor is important to the client's job performance. After determining its importance, the counselor may want to ascertain the client's specific behavior that reflects self-confidence. In essence, the three key words in evaluation procedures are adaptability, flexibility, and specificity.

It is important for the counselor to remember that when the client is experiencing difficulty on the job, the counselor has three major alternatives: (a) change the client, (b) change the job, or (c) change the employer. For example, an employer in a gas station stated that the client was not motivated and lacked initiative. The cilent said that he liked the job and wished to continue. Later it was found that the "nonmotivation" and "lack of initiative" were projected by the client's not smiling and by dragging his feet when he walked to a car. In fact, the soles of his shoes had holes in them and the heels were worn down. It would be possible to teach the client to maintain good posture, not drag his feet, and smile more while on the job. These would be ways to change the *client*. The client's *job* could be changed by requiring the client to pump gas on a night shift when it is permissible to walk slowly and look tired, or the client could find another occupation that would be more acceptable to his behaviors. Lastly, the *employer* could be changed. This refers to changing the employer's attitude or perspective on the situation. It could be explained to the employer that the client actually enjoys his job but comes from a home in which all of the family members drag their feet and do not smile. Some employers will accept this and continue to employ the client. Others will retain the client but alter his duties so he has less customer contact. Finally, there are employers who would say, "I don't care where he comes from. I just want him to pick up his feet, walk straight, and smile." With this type of employer, it may be feasible to place the client on another job under a different employer.

Conclusion

Evaluation and follow-up procedures were presented. The three-column evaluation sheet was suggested as a form that allowed the counselor to get more detailed information from the employer on how the client was performing. Next, an outline of possible evaluation factors was listed for the counselor to refer to in order to get the employer to discuss the client in more detail. Finally, it should be stated that no evaluation form or method is, by itself, an effective means of performing follow-up evaluations. Any tool, regardless of its origin, is only as good as the person using it. Aside from the personal characteristics that brings one to work in rehabilitation, we believe that the three key factors in evaluation procedures are adaptability, flexibility, and specificity.

References

Dubrow, M. On-the-job assistance. In The Woods Schools, *Outlook for the adult retarded.* Langhorne, Pa.: The Woods Schools, 1960.

Retarded youth: Their school rehabilitation needs. Research and Demonstration Project 681 sponsored by Minneapolis Public Schools, Federal Vocational Rehabilitation Administration, March 1965.

Scott, T. B., Dawis, R. V., England, G. W., & Lofquist, L. H. A definition of work adjustment. *Minnesota Studies in Vocational Rehabilitation,* 1960, *10*(30).

Chapter 8.

TELEPHONE: THE INITIAL CONTACT WITH EMPLOYERS

The plain everyday practice of talking on the telephone has the potential of becoming the most convenient and viable means of introducing the handicapped client to prospective employers. The telephone provides the opportunity for an expedient, direct, and immediate connection between the counselor and the employer. Used properly, following certain guidelines, the telephone can be the most powerful means of contacting the employer that the rehabilitation counselor or any counselor involved with placement has at his or her disposal. Used improperly, the telephone becomes a burden to the counselor and will result in contacts with prospective employers being lost or never attained.

The telephone has only two functions for the rehabilitation counselor: (a) it can be used to *set up an appointment,* or (b) it can be used to *obtain information*. Dubois (1976) stressed, "You can sell only one thing at a time. If you want an appointment, ask for the appointment. If you want information, ask for the information." (p.15-7) Never try to accomplish more than one objective per call. In other words, either ask for information or for an appointment but never ask for both in the same phone call.

At present there are many well-developed programs related to teaching individuals how to use the telephone properly. The three programs selected for adaptation to the needs of the rehabilitation counselor were developed by Nightengale (1975), Dubois (1976), and Meyer (1977). These three programs were selected because of their clarity and comprehensiveness, flexibility yet directness, as well as their applicability to the field of rehabilitation. The primary goal of this chapter is to share information on various telephone techniques and procedures that will assist the rehabilitation counselor in setting up potential employer appointments or to solicit vital information related to the employer, the employer's business, or future placement potential. To accomplish the goal of setting up an appointment or soliciting information, the topics of fear, mood, and specific approaches are explained and elaborated upon.

FEAR

The first thing the rehabilitation counselor has to overcome when using the phone is *fear*. Nightengale (1975) suggested the best way to overcome fear was to list the worst thing that could possibly happen on the initial phone call and then list several other things that could happen to instill fear into the person making the call. The worst thing would be if the employer hung up. Other things that could raise the counselor's anxiety or fear would be profanity or bad names, insults, loss of words, and objections. Just listing or knowing what causes fear gives the counselor a chance to understand and overcome fear.

Fear can also be generated by the anticipation of an employer's responding with no's. Dubois (1976) related this problem to army recruiters trying to overcome the fear of a prospect's no's. Adaptations are made to the suggestions offered by Dubois in order to come up with techniques for counselors to use in overcoming the no's of employers. To accomplish this, an understanding of the reason for the no's is necessary. There are four major reasons for the employer's no's:

1. A phone call is always an interruption to an employer.
2. Often counselors are not interesting over the phone.
3. The employer thinks the counselor will take too much of his or her time.
4. The employer is busy at the time the counselor is asking for an appointment.

(Adapted from Dubois, 1976, p. 15-1)

Mood

Although overcoming fear is important, equally important is the counselor's ability to become enthusiastic. The emotions and mood of the telephoning counselor directly affect the phone results. Before actually using the phone, it may be helpful to determine the counselor's *mood* or level of enthusiasm just prior to or at the time of the call.

There are several ways to become enthusiastic. Dubois (1976) suggested you boost your attitude and enthusiasm through animation: pep talks, rallies, singing in the shower, vigorous exercise, and so on. In order for the counselor to boost morale or mood, a list of three to five surefire ways of raising spirits should be listed. Simply write the self-suggestions down and do them. For example you might include eating breakfast at a restaurant, smiling at yourself in the mirror, listening to your favorite song (one counselor found that singing "Onward, Christian Soldiers" positively affected his telephone results).

A Counselor's Mood Meter was developed to assist the counselor in roughly evaluating the degree of enthusiasm or mood prior to or during the telephone procedure.

The counselor places an *X* in the cell(s) that represent the mood for that day. The Counselor's Mood Meter is read like a thermometer. The words in the top half of the chart indicate a good mood or attitude while the words in the lower half of the chart indicate that the mood and enthusiasm are down. The results of the phone calls are tabulated at the bottom of the chart. This allows the counselor to compare the results with the mood or level of enthusiasm. It has been found that in many cases the mood of the counselor directly affects the results of the phone

Figure 8-1. Counselor's Mood Meter.

Days	M	T	W	Th	F	S	S
Ecstatic							
Jubilant							
Elated							
Excited							
Joyful							
Purposeful							
Determined							
Full of Energy							
Ready to Go							
Satisfied							
Hesitant							
Worried							
Anxious							
Tired							
Frustrated							
Upset							
Down							
Miserable							
Number of Information Calls							
Number of Appointment Calls							
Number of Confirmed Appointments							

procedure, but more importantly, it has been found that counselors can positively influence their mood when they realize they are psychologically down. It is important to mention that once the counselor determines the reason(s) for failure, automatically the counselor's self-confidence increases. the more confidence the counselor acquires, the more motivated the counselor becomes (see Figure 8-1, Counselor's Mood Meter).

Approach

Once fear is understood and the mood or level of enthusiasm has been determined, the counselor is ready to formulate an *approach* or strategy for using the phone. The remainder of this chapter will explain the approach to be used and then elaborate on several components of the approach, including calling for an appointment, calling for information, and developing a telephone blueprint.

In general the approach should be geared toward one objective only. As mentioned earlier, the approach would have to be centered around calling for an appointment or calling for information but never both during the same phone call. Before calling the employer, the counselor needs to consider the following:

1. Get in a quiet room by yourself.
2. Set a time limit on how long you are going to use the phone (use 15 to 20 minutes at first).
3. Take a quick 2-or 3-minute break between calls.
4. Do not let anyone or anything disturb you (people, noise, radio, etc.).
5. Do not eat, drink, or smoke while talking on the telephone.
6. Psychologically, do not use the phone because you *need* an appointment; instead use the phone to help the employer *benefit* from your call by

offering the employer the opportunity to hire one of your clients. If you take this attitude you will feel more confident and it will come through in your voice.

According to Meyer (1977), when a person uses a telephone the prospect can judge the total force of your personality only through what is heard. The counselor needs to develop a telephone approach that will show genuine concern and interest. Meyers suggested the following:

1. Warm up before you make a phone call to prospective employers to avoid "cold calls." This can be accomplished by reading positive affirmations aloud. For example, "I am going to place Johnny Downs today!" "I will place or get an interview on this phone call!" By doing this you warm up the vocal cords, limber the lips and tongue, and at the same time build a positive mental attitude.
2. Establish a set time and place to use the telephone. Do not use it haphazardly or spasmodically. Set a planned amount of time that you are going to use the phone each day.
3. Develop a planned telephone approach with a blueprint or telechart of what you are going to say. Practice your planned approach until you sound professional.

Once the place and time for making phone calls has been selected, it is time to call for the purpose of making an appointment with the employer or to get information.

The Appointment

Dubois (1976) lists several advantages or benefits of making an appontment call, including the following:

1. Permits you to schedule your time more efficiently.
2. Helps assure the employer will see you when you come at the designated time.
3. Assures a more receptive attitude by the employer because you took the time to set up an appointment.
4. Prepares the employer for your visit.
5. Increases the quality of your approach as compared to when an appointment is not made.

Employers are busy people

One thing to keep in mind is that most employers are busy people, and a counselor should respect the employer's schedule. Dubois (1976) stated that 70 percent of the time an employer resists talking, it is simply because the employer happens to be really busy at that time. So first check to make sure the employer has time to talk (Ask the question "Am I taking you away from anything important?)" Second, when setting up an appointment time, ask for the appointment at odd times (9:50, 10:20, etc.). By using odd times, the counselor gives the employer the impression that not too much time is needed for the appointment. For example, when calling for an appointment:

Counselor: Mr. Smith, I'm ____ from _____ . Am I taking you away from anything important?

Employer: Yes, I'm very busy now.

Counselor: Oh! Excuse me, I'm sorry. Would it be better to call back later today or would you prefer tomorrow morning?

Employer: Call tomorrow morning.

Counselor: Would you prefer early or late morning?

Employer: Early, around eight thirty.

Counselor: Fine. Eight thirty it is. Thank you. Good-bye.

If the employer has time to talk, then the requested time for the personal appointment should be set at an off-hour time to imply that only a brief time for the appointment is needed.

Counselor: When would be a good time for me to drop by?

Would you prefer I come by this afternoon or would tomorrow be better?

Employer: Tomorrow.

Counselor: One twenty or three fifty p.m.?

Employer: Three fifty.

Counselor: Fine. I'll be there at three-fifty tomorrow.

Accept seven no's

Once the employer is on the phone, be ready to respond to his or her negative replies. Unfortunately, counselors many times give up after the first no. When calling for an appointment, it may be advisable not to give up until at least seven no's have been given. Dubois (1976) advised:

> Don't hang up after just one "no". People tend to get friendlier after the second or third "no". So, if you feel your ideas will benefit the prospect, relax and take a few "no's". If you don't get the appointment you don't get the opportunity to help the prospect. (p. 15-2)

For example:

Counselor: Mr. Smith, when would it be convenient to see you, today or tomorrow?

Employer: Neither. [First no]

Counselor: How about next week?

Employer: I am not sure. [Second no]

Counselor: Look at your schedule—do you have an opening for just five or ten minutes on Monday or Tuesday of next week?

Employer: Look, I'm busy. [Third no]

Counselor: Well, check for Monday afternoon.

Employer: No, I have a production meeting. [Fourth no]

Counselor: What about Tuesday morning?

Employer: No. [Fifth no]

Counselor: How about later in the week?

Employer: Don't you understand? I don't want to see you. [Sixth no]

Counselor: Yes, I understand. To tell you the truth, most

employers don't want to see me. Many hang up and leave me holding a dead line.

Employer: That's exactly what I'm going to do. [Seventh no]

Counselor: Mr. Smith, before you hang up let me say this. I can understand why *you* don't want to see me, but *I* want very much to see you. I have some ideas and some information that I feel you will be interested in and I assure you it will not be a waste of your time. Is there any way I can convince you to allow me to see you?

Employer: I'm not sure.

Counselor: Just tell me what I have to do. You name the time, anytime day or night.

Employer: Well, maybe next week.

Counselor: What day, Mr. Smith?

Employer: Tuesday.

Counselor: What time, Mr. Smith?

Employer: Nine a.m.

Counselor: Great. I'll be there Tuesday, nine a.m. on the dot. You won't be sorry. Good-bye.

From the above example it should be obvious that an effective way to overcome the negative response is not to ask questions that can be answered yes or no.

Do not ask yes or no questions

The easiest way to avoid the no or negative response is not to ask questions over the phone that can be answered with a yes or no. (The only exception to this is when the counselor determines if the employer is busy.) Give the employer a choice. For example, "Would ten twenty today or would two fifty tomorrow be a better time to see you?" Never ask if it would be convenient for you to see the employer. If you ask questions that can be answered yes or no you are no longer in control. Below are three illustrations of the wrong and right way to ask questions.

Wrong! Mr. Smith, could I come by to see you? [This can be answered yes or no.]

Right! Mr. Smith, may I come by to see you today or would tomorrow be better? [The employer is forced to make a choice, and if the employer does not want to see the counselor at least the employer has to tell the counselor in sentence form rather than with a quick no.]

Wrong! May I see you tomorrow? [Can be answered yes or no.]

Right! Would later today or tomorrow be best? [Cannot be answered yes or no.]

Wrong! Would you be interested in knowing more about our program? [Can be answered yes or no.]

Right! We have one of the top programs in the nation. What do I have to do to get an opportunity to personally tell you about it? [Cannot be answered yes or no.]

Tell them just a little

If employers keep insisting on more information when you are trying only to make an appointment, it may become necessary to give them just a preview of what you want to see them about. This can be handled by explaining briefly why they can benefit from an appointment with you. This is accomplished by making a *claim*, stating a *fact*, and then telling the employer how he or she will *benefit*. Finally, you may relate the *real benefit* to the employer if necessary. For example:

Employer: Well, tell me more about why I should see you.

Counselor: My agency can offer you personnel that are trained to fit into your organization [claim]. We have served several companies in the area [fact] and we can offer you some long-term prospects [benefit] for those jobs that you have trouble keeping personnel placed in [real benefit].

Never tell the employer more than is necessary to get the appointment. Remember the counselor's only objective is to get an appointment time. If the counselor tells everything trying to set up the appointment, then the employer's curiosity has probably been satisfied and an appointment may not be granted. Actually, a really professional placement specialist would stimulate the employer's curiosity by *first* calling for information, and *second*, on a later day, placing an appointment call.

INFORMATION CALL

The purpose of the information call is to stimulate the employer's curiosity. The information call is made to bait the hook, so to speak. The counselor should place the information call to attract the attention of the employer and to break the ice. The information call allows the counselor to establish contact with the employer *prior* to making an appointment call. This procedure eliminates the appointment calls being a cold canvas call.

The counselor would make the information call to raise the employer's curiosity. Then the counselor would call at a later date to ask for an appointment. The professional placement specialist knows calling back and asking for an appointment increases the possibility that the employer will be more receptive, since contact had already been made through the information call.

The technique the counselor should employ when making an information call is the *purpose-permission bridge*. The purpose of the call is explained briefly to the employer by the counselor; next the counselor receives permission, then three or four questions are asked the employer. The questions are designed to raise the employer's curiosity or to bait the hook for the appointment call, which will come in the next day or two. An example of using a *purpose-permission bridge* is in the blueprint below:

Counselor: dials number.

Employer: Hello, Smith here.

Counselor: Thank you, Mr. Smith. I have an idea you may be interested in. I am with the Vocational Rehabilitation Center here in town. My *purpose* at this time is to get your answers to a few questions so I can see if I can be of service to you. *Do you mind* if I ask them? [*Purpose-Permission bridge*]

Employer: I don't mind.

Counselor: Do you hire semiskilled people?

Employer: [Answers question]

Counselor: Are the employees in your organization assigned to semiskilled positions adequately trained?

Employer: [Answers question]

Counselor: Do you think longevity in semiskilled jobs is important?

Employer: [Answers question]

Counselor: Have semiskilled jobs in your organization been on the rise?

Employer: [Answers question]

Counselor: Thank you for the information. That is all the questions I have. I've got some exciting ideas running through my mind, but I want to do some more investigating. I'll call you later. [Hangs up]

If, when the counselor asks the employer for permission to talk, the employer is too busy at the time, the counselor should try to set a time to call back and get off the phone as quickly as possible. An example of a blueprint for an employer who is too busy would go something like this:

Counselor: Relaxes, dials number.

Employer: Hello.

Counselor: Mr. Smith, please.

Employer: Yes?

Counselor: Mr. Smith?

Employer: Yes.

Counselor: Thank you, Mr. Smith. I am with the Vocational Rehabilitation Center here in town. My purpose at this time is to get information so I can see if I can be of service to you. Am I taking you away from anything important?

Employer: Yes, I am very busy with interviews.

Counselor: Oh, I am sorry. When could I call back?

Employer: Tomorrow morning.

Counselor: About what time?

Employer: Ten a.m.

Counselor: Thanks, Mr. Smith. I'll call back at ten a.m. tomorrow. [hangs up]

Calling for information and calling for an appointment are crucial for a successful contact with employers. The constant and continuous practice of refining telephone skills and techniques will assist the counselor in increasing the number of appointments that are so vital to successful placement.

Conclusion

In this chapter telephoning techniques were developed for rehabilitation counselors or placement specialists from existing programs, teaching individuals involved in sales work or recruitment how to use the telephone effectively. Two functions or purposes involving rehabilitation counselors using the telephone were discussed. The two functions were to set up an appointment and to call for information. To accomplish these functions the topics of fear, mood, and specific approaches were elaborated on. Finally, specific examples of telephone conversations for making appointment calls and information calls were offered.

References

Dubois, L. *Creative selling instructors guide,* (USAMWRRC, Pamphlet No. 350-2). Fort Sheridan, Ill.: Department of the Army, United States Army, Midwestern Regional Recruiting Command, 1976.

Meyer, P. L. *Dynamics of creative selling.* Waco, Tex: Success Motivation Institute, 1977.

Nightengale, E. *Selling techniques that really work.* Chicago, Ill.: The Human Resource Ço., 1975.

Part III

ASSESSMENT AND DEVELOPMENT

Chapter 9

ASSESSMENT

Thus far, we have presented our views of the importance of formulating a personal philosophy on the nature of man in order to become more effective in working with people. Our explications of Graves's levels of existence speak directly to our appreciation of Dr. Graves's life work as a comprehensive model for understanding psychologically mature, healthy human behavior.

There are, of course, many other theories that we might have adopted, a few of which we used for the purposes of comparison and contrast in earlier chapters. A much more complete overview of such major theories has been provided by Loevinger (1976), and our study of this work has led us to conclude that while many of these theories offer views essentially similar to those of Graves, none of them appears to be as comprehensive. In fact, Dr. Graves contends that at least 43 other personality models can be covered, augmented, and explained by his theory. While such a claim is not to be taken lightly by serious behavioral scientists, Dr. Graves is not the first to have made it. He was preceded by Charles Darwin, Karl Marx, Sigmund Freud, and Marshall McLuhan, among others (Steed, 1968). But these latter names, and to some extent their viewpoints, are much more widely known than that of Clare Graves. And there must be a plausible explanation for this circumstance if his theory is, after all, as useful as we believe it is.

There are, in fact, several factors that have contributed to the relative obscurity of Dr. Graves's (1980) "Level of Existence, Emergent, Cyclical, Double Helix Model of Adult Human Psychosocial Coping Systems." One of these factors is implicit in the increased sophistication of the title of the theory. We know Dr. Graves to be a scientist in the purest sense of the word, and he has continued to develop his theory over the years through increasingly detailed analyses of his research data. He has told us of his reluctance to publish his work until he feels that the product will be fully representative of the complexities of his findings and their interpretations. He has also stated his concern about the many faulty interpretations of his views by overzealous followers and journal editors whose amplifications were not always accurate, regardless of their good intentions. His point is that while *their* views may be valid, they are not *his* views.

Dr. Graves also has been the victim of a number of events in recent years that have adversely affected his publication efforts, including retirement, ill health, and inadequate clerical assistance. He is, however, proceeding steadily and systematically toward publication of the totality of his work.

But as understanding as we are of his unfortunate circumstances, we remain hooked on the horns of a dilemma. We have presented in previous chapters a number of applications of Graves's theory, which we know to be effective. But fundamental to each of them is the capacity for classifying people into levels in some reliable way. Further, no theoretically specific instrument for the accomplishment of this task exists at the time of this writing; and this factor, probably more than any other, has contributed to the obscurity of the theory by seriously hampering research efforts.

EARLY DEVELOPMENTS[1]

According to Steed (1968), in the fall of 1952, Dr. Graves began his initial research, acting upon "a hunch":

> "All my life, I've been confused and perplexed by the fact that on every damned subject there are so many schools of thought. Take psychology. The whole field is a battleground of contrasting theories—the Freudians don't agree with the Adlerians, the psychoanalysts won't talk to the behaviorists. The same's true of all of life. Man is so confused that he speaks of peace—and then righteously makes war. He professes to care about poverty, but yet gives the poor so little that they riot. He advocates religious tolerance, yet we disapprove of interfaith marriages. Everywhere you look people are divided into rival factions, each group claiming that it is right and the others are wrong."
>
> Graves concluded that man is either just plain perverse, or there's been a colossal misconception underlying all previous theories of human personality. How else could you account for the fact that otherwise intelligent people persist in disagreeing on just about every subject? (p. 38)

This hunch has now come to be known as "The Level of Existence, Emergent, Cyclical, Double Helix Model of Adult Human Psychosocial Coping Systems."

Dr. Graves's research population was largely composed of students at Union College, Schenectady, New York, who ranged in age from 18 to 61 and included both men and women from a fairly widespread geographic area. During the first 5 weeks of each semester, students were asked to write their conceptions of psychologically mature, healthy human behavior; these were then gathered and classified into groups by a team of independent judges on the basis of similarities of answers. The resulting clas-

---

[1]Much of the historical information in this section is reported from a seminar, *Up the Existential Staircase*, conducted by Dr. Clare Graves in Chicago in August 1980.

sifications consisted of two major types of conceptions, which Dr. Graves called "express self type" and "sacrifice self type" because of the nature of their expressions. Each of these were further subdivided as follows:

Express Self Types

Express self—to Hell with others

Express self calculatedly, so as not to arouse the anger of others

Express self, but never at the expense of others

Sacrifice Self Types

Sacrifice self now to get later

Sacrifice self now to get now

Sacrifice self to the existential realities of which one is a part

During the second 5 weeks of each semester, the classes were divided into small groups of students who discussed their written conceptions among themselves. They were then asked to rewrite their conceptions based on their group critiquing experience, that their conceptions might reflect any modifications in views brought about by personal reconsideration and peer pressure. During the third 5 weeks of each semester, the already formed groups were instructed to develop a presentation of the views of various authorities in the field of human behavior, and then to rewrite, revise, or defend their conceptions in the light of the evidence available.

At the close of 7 years of this type of data collection, Dr. Graves had compiled 1,065 written conceptions of psychologically mature, healthy human behavior, which he began to study systematically. Dr. Graves found his data to be "quite confusing and confounding" at first, but persistent analysis brought forth some interesting patterns beyond the theoretical patterns themselves. Approximately 60 percent of the research population fell clearly into one of the major types, with 40 percent being a mixture of types. He noticed that if individual conceptions changed over time, they did so in a consistent and predictable way: express self conceptions became sacrifice self conceptions, and vice versa.

As Dr. Graves continued to study the conceptions, these changes became even more definitive, forming a human developmental schema that vacillated in viewpoint between the external world and attempts to change it, and the inner world and attempts to come to peace with it. The "express self—to Hell with others" conception, if changed, invariably became the "sacrifice self now to get later" conception. This latter conception, if changed, became the "express self calculatedly, so as not to arouse the anger of others" conception. The complete developmental sequence dictated by Graves's data is shown in Figure 9-1.

Graves believed that these conceptions were actually personality systems in miniature, and his ongoing study of them led to their descriptions as the discrete levels of existence presented earlier in this book, although many of the typological names we have used are not those preferred by Graves. We have presented the classification nomenclature most frequently found in the existing literature on Graves's theory which, according to Dr. Graves, was the creation of a well-meaning but misunderstanding editor of a journal that published one of his early articles. Figure 9-2 replaces the early conceptual themes of Figure 9-1 with the level descriptors currently used by Graves.

Figure 9-1. Developmental Sequence of Conception Changes.

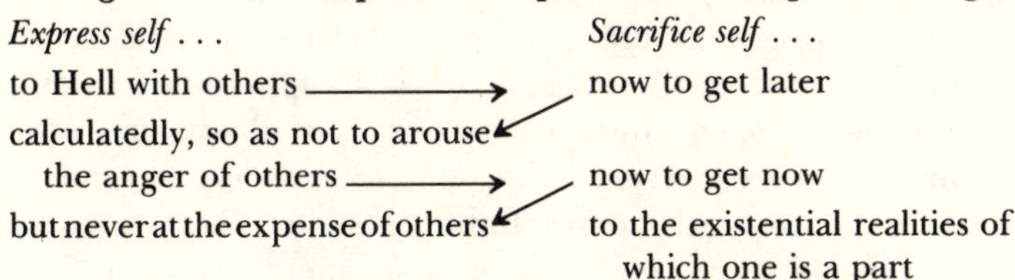

Another system not readily identifiable, but somewhere between express self and sacrifice self

Figure 9-2. Developmental Sequence of Levels of Existence.

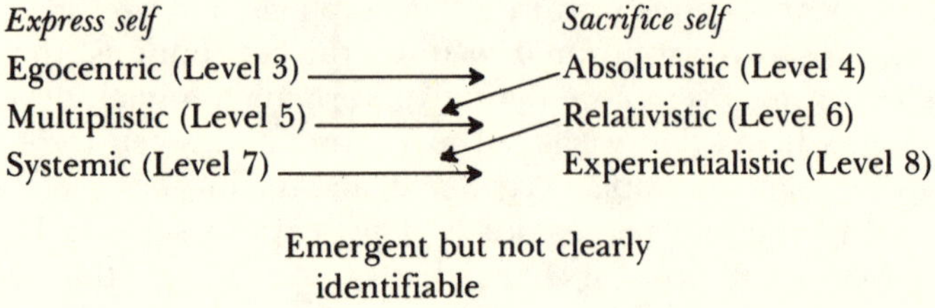

Express self		*Sacrifice self*
Egocentric (Level 3)	→	Absolutistic (Level 4)
Multiplistic (Level 5)	← →	Relativistic (Level 6)
Systemic (Level 7)	← →	Experientialistic (Level 8)

Emergent but not clearly identifiable

The earliest classification efforts, then, were performed by a team of independent judges following a strenuous process of writing, revising, and rewriting one's personal conceptions, with similar conceptions being grouped. While the method proved to be effective, Graves realized that a more direct method of assessing levels was necessary.

Level-Specific Classification Strategies

During the years of his data analysis, Dr. Graves noticed that certain words and phrases seemed to be more characteristic of some of the levels than of others. As his awareness of this circumstance increased, he developed a list of words wherein were embedded words to which each particular sytem would be sensitive. This list was then presented to subjects through the use of a tachistoscope at 1/100-second exposure, and the time of exposure progressively lengthened before the subject until recognition occurred. (A tachistoscope is an apparatus for testing attention, memory, etc., by throwing images of objects on a screen for a brief measured period, a fraction of a second.) This method proved to be most satisfactory, but it presented Dr. Graves with the second major parameter of his assessment problem. Stated simply, Dr. Graves still has the word list and it is still an effective classification tool, but once the list is published for assessment purposes it will quickly become invalid by reasons of transparency.

"THIS I BELIEVE" TEST[2]

Throughout our years of research, we have found the "This I Believe" Test (TIB) to be the single most reliable tool for constructing Graves's classification scheme. TIB arose from research reported by Harvey, Hunt, and Schroder (1961), in which four basic levels of human concreteness/abstractness, along with transitional stages, were deduced. Harvey (1966) devised the instrument as a means of measuring these basic thinking types, which he called "conceptual systems." Each of these theoretically based systems was defined by the way in which people's beliefs affected their interactions with their environments—that is, their behaviors.

Harvey (1966) has reported that TIB's "interjudge reliability for three and four trained judges in classifying subjects into one of the four main systems has been .90 or above for 12 different samples of subjects." (p. 47) He also reports test–retest reliabilities after 1 year in the range of .84–.90 (Harvey, 1979). Harvey (1966) presents the general results of several cross-validation efforts as substantiation for stating that the instrument has been "found in several studies to have high predictive and construct validity" (p. 46), although precise coefficients are not quoted. It should be noted, however, that many of the validity studies are included in technical reports for governmental studies that are not widely available.

Believing that he and Harvey were conducting somewhat parallel investigations of the same arena of human functioning (or ones quite similar), Graves consulted with Harvey about the possibility of adapting the TIB for use in classifying subjects into the levels of existence (Graves, 1979). Both men concluded that the TIB had established its utility in discriminating conceptual systems and that it could be used in researching Graves's theory by substituting Graves's level descriptors for Harvey's conceptual system descriptors. Because of the similarities in the focus of

---

[2]Much of the discussion here is taken from Hazlett (1980).

their research efforts, neither of the men thought that substitutions such as those proposed would affect the instrument's validity or reliability. Subsequently, Graves wrote guidelines for scoring the TIB according to the tenets of his theory (Graves, 1979; Harvey, 1979).

The TIB, of which we use an abbreviated form, requires participants to indicate their beliefs about such areas as friendship, sin, marriage, religion, people, rules, and the American way of life. The subjects' answers are then judged against the criteria that define the various psychological levels set forth by Graves, and are grouped by similarities of answers. Figure 9-3 presents the form of the TIB currently in use by us, and Figure 9-4 details Graves's scoring guidelines as compiled by the staff of the Management Center, University of Richmond, Richmond, Virginia, 1971.

We believe that one of the factors supportive of TIB's continuing successful use as an instrument for assessing Graves's

Figure 9-3. Opinion Survey.

INSTRUCTIONS—In the following questions you will be asked to write your opinions or beliefs about several topics. Please write *at least two* (2) sentences about each topic. Answer questions rapidly. You will be timed.

Be sure to write what you genuinely believe.

You must write on the topics in the order of their appearance.

1. This I believe about friendship.

2. This I believe about the American way of life.

3. This I believe about sin.

4. This I believe about marriage.

5. This I believe about religion.

6. This I believe about people.

7. This I believe about rules.

Figure 9-4. Bases for Scoring Opinion Survey According to Levels 3, 4, 5, and 6.

Do not score cliches, too short responses which give insufficient feeling or information.

Level 3—*The following are the bases for scoring responses as emanating from the Level 3 system.*

1. Any responses showing extreme sensitivity to external control or control by others.
2. Responses evidencing a tendency toward frequent blasts of hostility.
3. Perceiving the world in terms of imposition and control.
4. Responses which are highly egocentric and/or self-protective.
5. Responses showing a general lack of affective control.
6. Over-negative resistance to authority—any strong negativisim.
7. Attribution of malevolent purpose or intent to others.
8. Responses which defend the self—particularly defending self against critics.
9. Responses which are reactively and/or counteractively aggressive.
10. All or none responses which show others must either be all for me or they are against me.
11. Responses showing a strong negative feeling toward anyone or anything, as seen against the self doing as the self desires.
12. Responses showing no tolerance for ambiguity in that the person forcefully gets rid of the confusion by attack or by running away—leaving the field.
13. Responses showing no thoughtful consideration before acting, impulsivity, and solving by immediate simplistic action.

14. Responses which obviously avoid responding if the rest of the protocol is not Level 4.

Level 4—*The following are the bases for scoring responses as emanating from Level 4 thinking.*

1. Responses which interpret the world and its rules categorically and/or in terms of oughtness—ones which show the person feels rules ought to be obeyed without questioning their function or basis, responses which indicate rules, authority, etc., ought to be followed without question.

2. Responses which see the world, its people and all its things as under the control of divine fate.

3. Accepting what is at face value. No tendency to question if it comes from authority or on high.

4. Any response indicating a black–white interpretation of what is.

5. Responses which show "If it's right as I see the right, I accept it without question. If it is wrong, as I see, I reject it without question"—What is particularly noticeable here is when the respondent tends to give no indication of how he will determine right or wrong.

6. Response showing shame, guilt, or embarrassment as against ones showing anger. (This may be found in Level 6 systems—but let the totality of the response tell the tale.)

7. Answers which idealize parents, country, authority, etc., and which see parents, love of country, authority and the like as good and necessary.

8. Responses which show compliance with external authority and/or a recourse to authority in some form if and when dispute arises.

9. Responses which are deferential.

10. Responses which show an intolerance for ambiguity with recourse to authority in some form as the means for the removal

of it. (Note difference between Level 3 and Level 4, intolerance for ambiguity. Level 3 tries to banish it by attack, by driving it away, removing it by simplistic action, or running from it. Level 4 seeks recourse to authority to solve it.) (NOTE also that both Level 3's and Level 4's show immediate discomfort with ambiguity which differs from higher systems.)

11. Any response showing uncompromising compliance with an authority set, generalized standards—any showing of no alternative but to obeisance to higher status person.

12. Answers concerned positively with obeying, with doing it right, with being correct.

13. Responses showing an Authoritarian–Submissive character—that is, ones where what the respondent does depends on the status of who he sees telling him, ordering him, etc. Ones where he complies, agrees with the higher status and shows the opposite behavior to those of lower status.

Level 5—*The following provide the basic rationale for scoring responses as emanating from the Level 5 system.*

1. Responses which show a beginning, but a not too well developed tendency, to evaluate without the immediate and usually hostile negative rejection, though some negation is present. The former is Level 3. Ones which show tentative consideration before acceptance comes from authority. Immediate acceptance is Level 4. Nevertheless, the responses are more on the negative questioning side.

2. Responses showing some tendency, though not much, of the person to think in alternative ways unless it is authority to be rejected. Level 5's consider alternative ways, but always it is the self's best interest which determines the response (alternative) chosen.

3. Responses which begin to show the self are seen as distinct from the standard though not the complete and total selfishness at Level 3.

4. Tendency to look at things from more than one point of view with the self's empirically determined point of view prevailing.

5. Responses which show, "I'll do it if it is good for me or if I feel like it," accompanied by an appraisal of what is responded to. (NOTE:—out and out "I'll do it if I feel like it" are Level 3. Level 5's must distinguish some possibilities, and there must be conditionality.). (Note—Level 6's show even more conditionality and not the selfishness of Level 5's).

6. Responses showing tendency to want to express or to express anger in some modulated form. (Note: Level 4's suppress anger while Level 3's immediately express it, usually in raw physical form. Level 5 anger has some cognitive control in it).

7. Responses seeing authority figures, parents, rules, laws, etc. as necessary but restricting, as bugging or annoying, but not as malevolently intended, or imposing their will on respondent, as with the Level 3's.

8. Responses which snidely say, "What culture!!" "Who says there is a God," "You go to your church, I'll go to mine," or "You have your opinion, I have mine!"

9. Responses which say figuratively—"If I think I am right, I'll fight for my way."

10. Responses which negate the idea of a proper way of life, a national character, or culture.

11. A growing, not fully developed, ability to tolerate ambiguity, doubt, and the like—particularly those responses saying forcefully that self-chosen activity will be used to allay doubt. (Note: Level 4's turn to authority—Level 3's fight, or run—Level 5's self decide.)

12. Responses showing a negativistic tendency but with awareness of it, a tendency to control it but expressed in "I'll do it my way," or "I have my own free will which gives some consideration to rules etc., unless I feel they are not quite right and hamper me."

Level 6—*The following are the bases for scoring responses as Level 6 in character.*

1. Responses which see the world situationally, with many alternatives, each to his own, not too sure of his own tendency to follow his group of the moment. These responses are like the Level 7 system, but they lack the personal definitiveness of Level 7 systems.

2. Responses seeing and expressing many alternatives but choosing on the basis of feeling. (Note: Level 5's choose on basis of self-advantage, and Level 7's on basis of evidence).

3. Responses showing negative sensitiveness to control by authority, but positive sensitiveness to control by peer group.

4. Responses seeing self as distinct from the older generation, the general culture, but part of and loyal to peer group culture.

5. Responses showing tendency to criticize self and to want to change, not as the self or as authority desires, but as the group desires.

6. Rules, regulations, marriage and the like are necessary if not too strict or restricting. Rules and regulations should be minimized and changed with the situations.

7. Responses indicating parents, etc. have *their* way and we have *ours*.

8. Responses determined by feeling: "When I feel this way—I do this," or "When I feel that way, I do it that way."

9. Control is needed because if we don't have it, others might be hurt.

10. Responses reflecting the central importance of people, and particularly the people that one is associated with at the moment.

11. Responses reflecting a tendency to not have or to deny having negative feelings toward others.

12. Responses showing tendency not to initiate behavior or to have any beliefs that are contrary to the group associated with.

13. Responses showing a strong tendency toward a superficial approach to the world and its problems.

14. Responses bringing in relationships to people when not necessary.

15. Responses which indicate little or no tendency to actions that would hurt others.

16. Responses indicating "God's in his heaven, and all is right with the world." (NOTE: Level 4's would see *something* wrong!)

17. Responses saying, "I don't know it all, but I will fight for my friends' ways."

18. Accepting ambiguity but turning to friends or the group for clarification.

19. Friends are everything, are life, are living answers.

20. Marriage, my country, etc. are not perfect, not the best, but the best we have.

levels is its similarity to Graves's initial research method. It asks people to write what they believe about a particular thing or issue, and then people are grouped according to the similarities of their answers. But it too lacks sufficient power to discriminate clearly among the levels, owing largely to the complexity of human beings. Just as Piaget states that children's cognitive development may be uneven both across developmental stages and in depth regarding particular stages, Graves acknowledges that stages of adult development may also be uneven. For example, it is not uncommon to find TIB responses from a single individual that are level 6 (relativistic) in nature on the topics of friendship and people, while simultaneously reflecting level-5 (multiplistic) thinking about marriage and the American way of life and level-

4 (absolutistic) thinking about sin, religion, and rules. This exemplary mixture of responses is only one of the many combinations possible, owing to individual differences. The real question, according to Graves, is not at what level a person is functioning but rather at what level that person is operating in relation to a particular issue which he or she is trying to resolve. TIB is not sufficiently powerful to discern such intricate deviations.

FORCED-CHOICE "THIS I BELIEVE" TEST

From 1975 to 1977, James S. Payne and Ruth Ann Payne collected and analyzed more than 3,000 TIB responses in an effort to improve the instrument's utility. They had recognized TIB's inability to project system continuity from their years of experience in using the instrument. Each of the 3,000-plus responses to each TIB test item was recorded, classified according to Graves's guidelines, and then grouped on the basis of broad similarity. Frequency counts were then made of the recurring answers at each level, and the most frequently offered responses for each TIB item, by level, were chosen as exemplary level-specific statements.

In their research population, the Paynes found significant representation of Graves's levels 4 to 6, and evidence of level-7 thinking in a lesser number of instances. The Forced-Choice "This I Believe" Test (FCTIB) was constructed accordingly, allowing respondents to select three answers to each of the seven items on the TIB from among 14 possible choices: four level-4 (absolutistic) answers, four level-5 (multiplistic) answers, four level-6 (relativistic) answers, and two level-7 (systemic) answers. These choices have been randomized throughout the response sets, and scoring is accomplished by means of an overlay scoring key. The twenty-one resulting responses are grouped by level and displayed in tabular form, as in Figure 9-5, to show the relative level-specific valence of the respondent.

In this particular instance, a respondent identified with a significantly larger number of level-4 (absolutistic) statements

Figure 9.5. TIBFC Relative Valence of Respondent.

Type of Response	4	5	6	7
Response Frequency	14	4	3	0

than any of the others. This doesn't brand the person as a "Level 4," but rather, his apparent preference for absolutistic thinking provides us with a wealth of information about how we can best establish a sound and effective communication relationship with him.

The FCTIB has been used only as an informal device, often administered immediately after the TIB (in order to avoid prejudicial effects) as a means of concurrent validation of the TIB answers. Our use of FCTIB in this way has produced satisfying results, yielding correlations with TIB in the .60–.70 range. But as helpful as it may be, FCTIB falls woefully short of being the reliable and valid instrument necessary for assessing Graves's levels, and we would recommend its use in its present form only as an informal indicator for demonstration purposes. Figure 9-6 presents the items and response sets of the FCTIB.

Other Research

For a number of years, the significance of the assessment problems has occupied much of the time and effort of proponents of the level of existence point of view. Among those who have been most active are Drs. Vincent Flowers and Charles Hughes of the Center for Values Analysis in Richardson, Texas, who have worked intensively at constructing various instruments consistent with their interpretations of the theory. Susan and Scott Myers have contributed much to industrial applications of the levels of existence and have amassed a wealth of useful survey data. The staff of the University of Richmond's Institute for Business and Community Development has conducted numerous seminars that offer their interpretations and applications of the viewpoint. Dr. Don Beck founded the National Values Center

Figure 9.6. Opinion Survey.

INSTRUCTIONS—In the following questions you are asked to select your opinions or beliefs about seven topics. Each of the seven topics has 14 choices. You are requested to read all 14 choices and select three that most closely reflect your opinion or belief. Read and answer the questions rapidly; you will be timed, but since there are no right or wrong answers, be sure to read all the responses before making your choice.

Be sure to select those choices that most genuinely characterize your beliefs.

You must respond to topics in order of their appearance.

THIS I BELIEVE ABOUT FRIENDSHIP.

A. It is a lasting and permanent relationship.

B. Necessary commodity for existence.

C. Most important human relation.

D. A changing thing with time.

E. Mechanism of self growth.

F. Weak people need more friends than independent people.

G. Women make the worst friends.

H. Give and take process.

I. A mate without sex.

J. More valuable than money.

K. Sacred and binding.

L. Friends are gifts to yourself.

M. Without friends life is nothing.

N. Some people need friends, some people don't.

THIS I BELIEVE ABOUT THE AMERICAN WAY OF LIFE.

A. Something to be treasured and generally gives people a chance to live as they want.

B. McDonald's is taking over.

C. I'm the American way of life—I believe in myself.

D. Equal opportunity for everyone.

E. Opportunistic if you know how to get what you want.

F. People killing themselves to outdo one another.

G. Competition has brought about highest standard of living ever achieved in history.

H. Church, Mom, apple pie, Best I've ever tried.

I. Far from perfect but still the best in the world.

J. Decent way of life.

K. People being pushed to believe in power and money rather than more important things.

L. Confused society with misplaced values.

M. Love it—even with its imperfections, impurities and contradictions.

N. Old concept that does not hold anymore and as far as I'm concerned shouldn't hold anymore.

THIS I BELIEVE ABOUT SIN

A. There are no levels of sin—wrong is wrong.

B. A natural phenomenon.

C. Sin is everywhere.

D. What you feel it is; not what the church dictates.

E. A wrong against God and myself.

F. It is personal, not what society dictates.

G. God forgives sin "large" or "small."

H. Something you are forced to do against your better judgment.

I. Sin is learned.

J. No such thing, dreamed up to scare people.

K. Exists in mental state.

L. Will always be somewhere.

M. Something that goes against the thought of God.

N. Different people consider different things sin.

THIS I BELIEVE ABOUT MARRIAGE.

A. It is beautiful and lasts when it is God centered.

B. Marriage is a trial and error method toward eventual happiness.

C. A state of mind, not a piece of paper.

D. A way to insure that both partners try harder to stay together.

E. Necessary institution, if only to raise children properly.

F. Sacred union of two people who love each other and should be faithful to one another.

G. Costs a lot of money.

H. Necessary to raise children; otherwise you can just live together.

I. A sacred and fragile relationship with another person.

J. Social institution that corrupts a lot of relationships.

K. Good for some, bad for others.

L. Should be a constant love affair.

M. Spiritual and physical union between 2 people.

THIS I BELIEVE ABOUT RELIGION.

A. As necessary as marriage to a culture.

B. Gives a reason for living.

C. Is necessary for living a full and meaningful life.

D. Is very important to me.

E. Is interesting and is important to many people.

F. Devotion to a thought of a higher power than can control life.

G. People generally need someone or something to believe in.

H. Based on firm belief and faith and should be practiced often by frequently attending church services.

I. Don't see how people get so involved with it.

J. Don't have to go to church to have religion or to believe in God.

K. Religion is relative: it can help or hinder in life.

L. Religion is becoming too commercial.

M. Modern man has taken the faith out of religion.

N. Believe in God and abide in him and he will give you joy and happiness.

THIS I BELIEVE ABOUT PEOPLE.

A. Without people life is nothing.

B. People are basically no good, but I love them anyway.

C. People are of one creation.

D. Must learn to be themselves—honest and open.

E. People need other people.

F. A lot of people are virtually worthless; when dead, they are easily forgotten.

G. People are beautiful, but even beautiful people shit.

H. Can improve by opening up and sharing more with each other so that everyone can get most out of life.

I. I need people around to feel happy and secure.

J. Can't be trusted.

K. People as I see them are beautiful, if only the world could be beautiful with all those people.

L. They are very unpredictable, half animal at times.

M. People need each other.

N. They are the most unique set of organisms in the world.

THIS I BELIEVE ABOUT RULES

A. Some people like them, some people need them, a few people hate them.

B. Too much emphasis on them.

C. Can be good organizing tool.

D. Stifle creativity.

E. Rules are guidelines.

F. Necessary for social order.

G. There is nothing wrong with good rules.

H. Necessary in any situation.

I. Some are prejudice against some people.

J. If you break them you should expect punishment.

K. Useful if reasonable.

L. I can take them or leave them, but I try to obey most of the important rules.

M. Are made to be obeyed.

N. Rules are inconsistent.

in Dallas to further study and promote the theory, and he has worked quite closely in recent years with Dr. Graves himself. The authors, along with many others who have been in some way affiliated with the University of Virginia, have been engaged in training, research, and consultation activities revolving around the theory for nearly a decade now, with this chapter being one of our interim products.

In short, we know that a multitude of approaches have been formulated to resolve the problem of directly assessing Graves's levels. Many instruments have been constructed (sometimes with an attitude of near desperation), to say nothing of the endless search for existent and well-standardized personality inventories, attitude surveys, and the like (in seemingly never-ending combinations) that might meet the need. We also know that a number of research approaches have been undertaken for testing the theory's hypotheses and their worth for applications across a number of disciplines. But while we continue to make interesting discoveries, we remain relatively distant from a satisfactorily valid and reliable assessment instrument.

Needed Research

Obviously, we must continue efforts toward widespread classification capability if the theory is to realize its apparent potential. In Dr. Graves's most recent (1980) series of seminars entitled "Up the Existential Staircase," he set forth what he believes are the four possible ways of assessing people according to his premises:

1. *Presentation of system-specific stimuli*

Since each system is sensitive to specific stimuli, subjects might be presented with controlled, system-specific stimuli wherefrom the nature of the response indicates the individual differences in sensitization to the system represented by the stimuli. Dr. Graves believes this to be the best assessment method, and it is the same that we described earlier under the heading Level-specific Classification Strategies.

2. *Research assessment*

Another method that might be employed is to present system-relevant stimuli in a situation that requires some action, noting the congruity of the behavior with that expected based on theoretical premises. Needless to say, this method would not be practical for large-scale applications.

3. *Clinical method*

Dr. Graves believes that a very good method of assessment is the presentation of many stimuli, some of which are specifically related to a system and some of which are related to another system, noting which of the stimuli leads to affective arousal and the type of arousal that is produced. This method would be most difficult to perform because of its complexities, required equipment, and other costs, as well as its potential ethical implications.

4. *Practical method*

This final method involves the presentation of relatively ambiguous stimuli from which differences in interpretation of those ambiguous stimuli would serve to reflect the subject's systemic disposition. Use of TIB, as we have described it, would approximate such a method; and in chapter 10, we have presented research performed by Hazlett (1980) that relates the results of such an application to respondent profile scores on the California Psychological Inventory.

References

Graves, C. W. Personal communication, March 14, 1979.

Graves, C. W. *Up the existential staircase.* Dallas, Author, 1980.

Harvey, O. J. *Experience Structure and Adaptability.* New York: Springer, 1966.

Harvey, O. J. Personal communication, March 24, 1979.

Harvey, O. J., Hunt, D. E., & Schroder, H. M. *Conceptual systems and personality organization.* New York: John Wiley, 1961.

Hazlett, R. L. Levels of existence: A values-based approach to human motivation and management (doctoral dissertation, University of Virginia, 1980). *Dissertation Abstracts International,* 1980, *41,* 3617B. (Microfilm No. 8027953)

Leovinger, J. & Wessler, R. *Measuring Ego-Development* (2nd ed.) San Francisco: Jossey Bass, Inc., 1978.

Management Center, University of Richmond. *Graves' Levels of Existence.* Richmond, Va: 1971.

Steed, N. Every once in a while, there comes along a theory that explains everything. *Cavalier,* 1968, *18*(4), 37–40; 81.

Chapter 10

APPLICATION AND EXPLORATIONS OF THE PRACTICAL ASSESSMENT METHOD[1]

Statement of the Problem

The research reported here was prompted by the increasingly adversarial nature of labor-management relations in recent years. Hazlett views this situation as an indication of the existence of a gap between theory development and theory utilization, a breach that he further believes might be at least partially attributable to the embracement of differing notions about human nature. For example, while convincing data and arguments exist in support of both Theory X and Theory Y management assumptions, additional data indicate that neither Theory X nor Theory Y is effective when applied exclusively (Gellerman, 1968). Rather, the most effective approach to sustained productivity appears to be a mixed or flexible style of management that continually adapts itself to changing conditions. As Behling and Shapiro (1974) put it, "The wide variety of incentives to which

---

[1]Portions of this chapter are excerpted from Hazlett (1980).

individuals respond clearly indicates the need for a theory based upon the possibility that almost anything can act as an incentive for greater work effort." (p. 62)

Dr. Graves believes that such differences are the result of varying needs and values. If Graves is to be believed, Hazlett felt that it should be possible to find people who share many common needs, values, and traits, and to classify them accordingly. Each of these "levels," then, should suggest specific techniques for motivating and managing the people who had been so categorized.

Approach to the Problem

Hazlett's research was based on what may be conceived of as two of Graves's fundamental theoretical assertions. The first of these is that people who have been classified at each of his levels will possess distinct personality characteristics that serve to differentiate them from representatives of other levels. The second is that if each state has discrete attributes, then the people classified at a given level should be more like each other than they are like representatives of other levels; that is, there should be a significant degree of homogeneity among them. Hazlett conceded, however, that he was unlikely to find representatives of all of Graves's levels in any given and readily accessible research population. He expected not to find representatives of levels 1, 2, 8, and perhaps 3 and 7. While acknowledging that a more limited research focus dictated caution in generalizing the results, he thought that his research would attempt to tap those levels (4 to 6) that comprise approximately 70 percent of the adult population of our society (Flowers & Hughes, 1976).

Hypotheses

On the basis of Graves's theory then, nine hypotheses were derived to be subjected to empirical test.

First of all, the theory implies that levels of existence entail qualitatively different world views and probable social responses. It follows that individuals who are at the same level will be more homogeneous in their personality makeups than those at different levels. For example, level-4 individuals should tend to resemble other level 4's more closely across a variety of traits than they do people at any other level. For any extensive sampling of the personality domain, within-level homogeneity should exceed between-level homogeneity.

Second, saintly/conformist people (level 4's), because of their emphasis on what they "ought to" do, should evidence a higher sense of responsibility than level 5's, whose behavior is governed more by potential self-gain than by principle.

Third, because their behavior is characterized by self-denial, deference, and harsh self-discipline, level 4's should evidence a greater degree of self-control than their manipulative, opportunistic, and more impulsive counterparts at level 5.

Fourth, because saintly people value and adhere to structure and organization, their achievement efforts should be governed more by standards of conformance than will be true of level 6's, who are generally rebellious toward imposed standards perceived as restrictive to individuality.

Fifth, politically minded, socially ascendant, wheeler-dealer level 5's should exhibit more social presence than level 4's, who do not value such behaviors.

Sixth, level 5's should evidence a greater degree of self-acceptance than will level 4's, since materialism, manipulation, and assertive individuality seem to be more prized in our society than persevering self-control.

Seventh, the more relaxed and easygoing level 6's should evidence more tolerance than the more rigid, controlled level 4's.

Eighth, for many of the reasons already cited, level-6 people should evidence a higher level of flexibility than will level 4's.

Finally, since the traits most often ascribed to level-6 people are those that have traditionally been associated with femininity, sociocentrics should evidence more feminine behaviors than the historically more masculinely described level 5's.

METHOD

Subjects

Participants in this study were 86 employed professionals from seven Middle Atlantic States who were enrolled by their employers in an in-service training program on aspects of vocational counseling. They ranged in age from 22 to 58 years and were composed of 46 women and 40 men. The racial makeup of the group was 74.4 percent white, 22.1 percent black, and 3.5 percent other minorities.

Educationally, the subjects ranged from high school graduates (1.2 percent) to those possessing advanced degrees, masters level and beyond (44.2 percent). The clear majority of participants (51.2 percent) were employed in urban settings, and 60 of them were employed in counseling positions. The remainder were employed in various guidance and supporting roles (e.g., instructors, aides, specialists, supervisors, testers). Selection of individuals for participation in the training program was beyond the control of the experimenter, and all trainees were tested except those who were physically unable to perform the procedures required of them because of a handicapping condition (e.g., the visually impaired).

Measures

Two instruments were employed in the study, the "This I Believe" Test (TIB) for classifying subjects into Graves's levels and the California Psychological Inventory (CPI) for collecting necessary data on personality characteristics.

The CPI scales selected for testing the hypotheses of the study, along with their statements of purpose, were

Re (Responsibility)—to identify persons of conscientious, responsible, and dependable disposition and temperament.

Sc (Self-control)—to assess the degree and adequacy of self-regulation and self-control and freedom from impulsivity and self-centeredness.

Ac (Achievement via conformance)—to identify those factors of interest and motivation that facilitate achievement in any setting where conformance is a positive behavior.

Sp (Social presence)—to assess factors such as poise, spontaneity, and self-confidence in personal and social interaction.

Sa (Self-acceptance)—to assess factors such as sense of personal worth, self-acceptance, and capacity for independent thinking and action.

To (Tolerance)—to identify persons with permissive, accepting, and nonjudgmental social beliefs and attitudes.

Fx (Flexibility)—to indicate the degree of flexibility and adaptability of a person's thinking and social behavior.

Fe (Femininity)—to assess the masculinity or femininity of interests. (High scores indicate more feminine interests, low scores more masculine). (Gough, 1975, pp. 10–11)

Procedures

Testing. Subjects were tested in groups of approximately 15, requiring 6 administrations of approximately 1¾ hours duration. The self-administering instruments were distributed to the subjects in random fashion, with approximately one-half of the participants completing the TIB first and the remainder completing the CPI first. The distribution pattern was then reversed for completing the administration.

Since the information being sought was of an intimate nature, participants were instructed to devise a symbol (e.g., star, square, etc.) or other distinctive mark to be used on all test materials as a substitute for actual names. These symbols preserved the anonymity of individual participants, thereby encouraging more honest responses.

Upon completing each administration, all materials were checked for compliance with directions, nonduplication of symbols, and so on. Two sets of duplicate symbols were found, and arbitrarily chosen subscripts were added to the duplicate for future differentiation. Both the TIB and the CPI were hand-scored, the latter by means of stencils supplied by its publisher and the former according to Graves's guidelines. Participants' answers on the CPI were then dichotomously coded, "true" answers being given the value 1 and "false" answers being coded 0.

Classification. The grouping of people at distinct levels, according to Graves's formulations, was ascertained directly by scoring the TIBs. Duplicate sets of the instruments were independently scored by three authorities on Graves's theory. Any sets of TIB responses that could not be classified unanimously by the judges because of the openness of the responses were discarded from further analysis.

In general, the interrater reliability proved to be satisfactory across the three judges (Spearman-Brown–corrected reliability was .80). As would be expected on theoretical grounds, no one was found at levels 1, 2, 3, or 8; only four individuals were found at level 7. A breakdown of the number of individuals found at each level is shown in Table 10-1.

Having completed the task of classifying the subjects into Graves's levels, their CPI data were subjected to several statistical treatments and analyses to test the study's hypotheses.

Table 10-1.
Distribution of Sample by Level of Existence

Level	*Number of cases*
4 (Saintly)	22
5 (Materialistic)	30
6 (Sociocentric)	20
7 (Cognitive)	4
Unclassified*	10
Total	86

*The unclassified category represents those participants whose classification could not be decided unanimously.

RESULTS

This section has been divided into two major subsections. The analyses and outcomes associated with testing the homogeneity hypothesis are presented first. The first major subsection has been further subdivided into two analyses: Analysis 1 provides a direct test of the hypothesis that subjects within levels will be more alike in their CPI responding than subjects between levels; Analysis 2 is used to estimate the degree of fit between the TIB classification system and empirically derived factors from the CPI data. Finally, in the second major subsection, descriptive data and statistical tests of the hypotheses of mean differences among levels are presented.

Homogeneity Hypothesis Testing

Analysis 1. Since one of Graves's tenets is that most people are a mixture of two or more levels, only the five clearest exemplars of each level were chosen, in order to provide a more cogent test of the homogeneity hypothesis. This was done by consulting the classifications of the raters and eliminating all those participants at each level who were labeled "open" and those for whom multiple levels were reported. The participant numbers of the remaining subjects were then placed in a container and numbers were drawn until the new subsets of the sample were formed. These new groups were named Model (level 4), Prototype (level 5), and Stereotype (level 6) to differentiate them from the total sample in the reporting of results.

Having selected the data base for the first analysis, the participants' CPI data were transposed, creating a 480-by-15 matrix (the number of CPI responses by the number of respondents). From these data, a 15-by-15 matrix of *G* indices of agreement (Holley, 1964; Holley & Guilford, 1964) as generated. The *G* statistic is based on the simple probability of agreement of responses. Therefore, the higher the *G* index value the more similar the response patterns. The matrix just created, then, may properly be called a matrix of interpersonal similarity coefficients, although these *G* indices should not be regarded as being true correlations.

After performing these preliminary data transformations, the *G* coefficients were rank-ordered on the basis of magnitude, and a rank order test (Mann-Whitney *U*) was conducted to test the hypothesis that subjects within levels were more alike than subjects between levels. The results of these analyses are shown in Tables 10-2 and 10-3, with Table 10-2 reproducing the matrix of interpersonal similarity coefficients reported to four decimal places to avoid ties in rank ordering. Table 10-3 displays the results of rank ordering of the *G* indices, wherein the Mann-Whitney *U* test proved to be significant ($U = 206$; $p < .001$).

The rank order of *G* coefficients obtains additional clarity when displayed graphically as in Table 10-4. This table is a reformulation of Table 10-3 wherein notations for same level and different level representation have been substituted for the computed *G* indices.

These results provide strong evidence in support of the hypothesis that people who are classified at the same level of existence are more alike than those who are categorized at different levels. In addition, the testing procedures utilized have important implications for other "stage" theories, a topic that will be more fully explored presently.

Analysis 2. This second analysis is a logical extension of the first one, having as its goal the estimation of the degree of concordance between the TIB-based classification system and empirically derived factors from the CPI data.

The matrix of interpersonal similarity coefficients shown in Table 10-2 were subjected to a principal components factor analysis, and a scree test was conducted. This test suggested the existence of three interpretable factors, which is consistent with the belief that there would be three distinct types of people. The factors were rotated according to the Oblimin Criterion, and the resulting factor loadings are shown in Table 10-5. Also shown in Table 10-5 are the loadings that would be expected on the

Table 10-2.
Matrix of Interpersonal Similarity Coefficients for Closed Personality Types at Levels 4, 5, and 6

	Level														
			4					*5*					*6*		
Subject	*4*	*20*	*36*	*71*	*80*	*28*	*32*	*43*	*60*	*83*	*46*	*48*	*51*	*59*	*74*
4															
20	.3892														
36	.4425	.3922													
71	.4642	.3753	.4800												
80	.3367	.3960	.4488	.3680											
28	.2525	.1917	.2851	.2872	.2855										
32	.2815	.2230	.2559	.3116	.2810	.3713									
43	.3115	.3023	.2839	.3727	.3016	.3945	.3509								
60	.2308	.2317	.2919	.2747	.2556	.4402	.3934	.3851							
83	.2214	.2382	.1989	.2526	.3139	.4558	.4351	.4009	.4351						
46	.2808	.3594	.3634	.2706	.3224	.3934	.3580	.4224	.3406	.3908					
48	.1501	.1981	.2708	.1279	.2701	.2605	.2799	.1587	.3146	.3040	.2946				
51	.1937	.2160	.3264	.2801	.2788	.4112	.2886	.2906	.2625	.3387	.4285	.4285			
59	.2101	.2913	.3612	.2906	.3466	.3505	.2598	.3171	.3027	.3269	.3419	.4038	.3153		
74	.2253	.1883	.3042	.3115	.3554	.3971	.3140	.2768	.3579	.4435	.3500	.3861	.3590	.3274	

Table 10-3.
Rank Order of Interpersonal Similarity Coefficients for Closed Personality Types at Levels 4, 5, and 6*

	10	*9*	*8*	*7*	*6*	*5*	*4*	*3*	*2*	*1*
100						.4800**	.4642	.4558	.4488	.4435
90	.4425	.4402	.4351	.4351	.4285	.4285	.4224	.4112	.4038	.4009
80	.3971	.3960	.3945	.3934	.3934	.3922	.3908	.3892	.3861	.3851
70	.3753	.3727	.3712	.3680	.3634	.3612	.3594	.3590	.3580	.3579
60	.3554	.3509	.3505	.3500	.3466	.3419	.3406	.3387	.3367	.3274
50	.3269	.3264	.3224	.3171	.3153	.3146	.3140	.3139	.3116	.3115
40	.3115	.3042	.3040	.3027	.3023	.3016	.2946	.2919	.2913	.2906
30	.2906	.2886	.2872	.2855	.2851	.2839	.2815	.2810	.2808	.2801
20	.2799	.2788	.2768	.2747	.2708	.2706	.2701	.2626	.2605	.2598
10	.2559	.2556	.2526	.2525	.2382	.2317	.2308	.2253	.2230	.2214
0	.2160	.2101	.1989	.1981	.1937	.1917	.1883	.1587	.1501	.1279

*Rank order is indicated for a given entry by adding column and row designations.
**Four decimal places are reported to avoid ties in rank ordering.

Table 10-4.
Level of Existence Representation by Rank Order of Interpersonal Similarity Coefficients*

	10	*9*	*8*	*7*	*6*	*5*	*4*	*3*	*2*	*1*
100						S	S	S	S	—
90	S	S	S	S	S	S	—	—	S	S
80	—	S	S	S	—	S	—	S	S	S
70	S	—	S	S	—	—	—	S	—	—
60	—	S	—	S	—	S	—	—	S	S
50	—	—	—	—	S	—	—	—	—	—
40	—	—	—	—	—	—	S	—	—	—
30	—	—	—	—	—	—	—	—	—	—
20	—	—	—	—	—	—	—	—	—	—
10	—	—	—	—	—	—	—	—	—	—
0	—	—	—	—	—	—	—	—	—	—

*S indicates that entry is representative of same level pairs of individuals; a dash indicates that entry is representative of different levels. Rank order is indicated for a given entry by adding column and row designations.

basis of Graves's theory if both the TIB procedures and CPI measures were error-free.

Table 10-5 shows clearly that there is considerable congruence between the TIB classification system and the factors that were empirically derived from the subjects' CPI data. In order to ascertain more precisely the degree of fit between these data, however, coefficients of factorial similarity were computed (Harman, 1968) and are displayed in Table 10-6. Coefficients of the magnitude shown indicate that with only a single exception, the 15 subjects were perfectly classified on the basis of highest-factor loading.

An additional finding of interest emerged from intercorrelating the three empirically derived factors. This procedure clearly revealed that adjacent levels correlated more highly with each other than did levels that were one apart ($r_{I,II} = .45$; $r_{I,III} = .28$; $r_{II,III} = .39$). This is precisely the situation that would be hoped for as evidence that a particular stage theory is developmental in nature, and the analytic procedure that revealed it thus has implications for investigation of other stage theories.

Table 10-5.
Rotated Factor Loadings for Principal Component Factor Analysis of Interpersonal Similarity Coefficients

	Predicted Loadings			*Oblique Factor Loadings*		
Subject	*I*	*II*	*III*	*I*	*II*	*III*
4	1	0	0	.74*	.10	−.18
20	1	0	0	.71*	−.04	.05
36	1	0	0	.74*	−.11	.24
71	1	0	0	.70*	.16	−.12
80	1	0	0	.57*	.00	.27
28	0	1	0	−.04	.69*	.13
32	0	1	0	.05	.68*	−.03
43	0	1	0	.23	.67*	−.20
60	0	1	0	−.02	.70*	.05
83	0	1	0	−.11	.76*	.11
46	0	0	1	.20	.41*	.22
48	0	0	1	−.03	.01	.83*
51	0	0	1	.07	.21	.57*
59	0	0	1	.24	.09	.53*
74	0	0	1	.04	.37*	.43*

*Loading greater than .30.

Table 10-6.[a]
Coefficients of Factorial Similarity Between Predicted and Actual Loadings*

	I	*II*	*III*
I	.96	.03	.09
II	.03	.93	.02
III	.14	.29	.86

[a]Harman, 1968.
*Primes are predicted loadings.

Having discovered that there were differences among the three distinct, homogeneous groups constructed by the TIB, the remaining analyses were structured to provide more information about the sources of those differences and their relationship to the study's directional hypotheses.

Hypotheses of Mean Differences

In order to see if there were significant differences overall among the mean CPI scores of all 72 classifiable subjects by level, a multivariate analysis of variance was performed. The results of this procedure are shown in Table 10-7. A multivariate test of significance for the effect of level of existence on the criterion variables was significant (Wilks' Lambda, $F = 2.05$, $p < .003$).

The presence of significant mean score differences overall thus suggested the conduct of a univariate analysis of variance for ascertaining the specific criterion variables that accounted for the differences. These were then compared with the level-specific differences specified by *a priori* contrasts. Table 10-8 displays the univariate F-tests results and Table 10-9 shows the *a priori* contrasts.

As may be seen from Table 10-8, the F ratios for six of the criterion variables (i.e., Sy, Sp, Sa, Re, Sc, and Gi) were significant ($p < .05$). On an additional variable, Fx, the F ratio approached, but did not achieve, the established significance level. Variables specified in *a priori* contrasts (Table 10-9) accounted for more than 57 percent of the variables that were found to have significant F ratios. In spite of the fact that all of the variables that were forecast to exhibit level-specific differences did not achieve the criterion significance level, Table 10-9 shows that all predictions were directionally accurate.

Because of the presence of a mixture of levels in the sample, the simple analysis of variance procedure was repeated on the data supplied by the 15 level exemplars who were utilized in the testing of the homogeneity hypothesis. The univariate F-tests results for this group are presented in Table 10-10, and the a priori contrasts results are displayed in Table 10-11.

Table 10-7.
Multivariate Analysis of Variance Cell Means and Standard Deviations for Level of Existence by CPI Scores

	Level of Existence							
	*4**		*5***		*6†*		*Sample‡*	
Variate	*Mean*	*SD*	*Mean*	*SD*	*Mean*	*SD*	*Mean*	*SD*
Do	27.95	4.27	28.57	6.40	28.80	5.30	28.44	5.45
Cs	18.91	3.83	20.80	2.89	20.75	3.57	20.21	3.45
Sy	22.82	4.53	26.57	4.30	24.30	5.06	24.79	4.81
Sp	33.64	7.46	41.07	5.63	38.55	4.30	38.10	6.65
Sa	20.14	3.43	24.03	3.23	22.70	3.81	22.47	3.79
Wb	35.73	6.24	36.40	4.04	35.60	4.17	35.97	4.79
Re	32.36	3.63	26.67	3.44	27.90	4.48	28.75	4.49
So	36.77	5.12	36.63	4.24	34.30	3.77	36.03	4.48
Sc	32.91	8.29	27.53	6.36	27.05	6.65	29.04	7.44
To	22.05	4.47	23.17	4.47	23.80	3.87	23.00	4.31
Gi	18.68	5.92	14.67	6.33	13.55	5.77	15.58	6.34
Cm	26.50	1.50	26.23	1.98	25.90	1.83	26.22	1.79
Ac	29.05	3.39	28.17	3.71	27.60	3.15	28.28	3.46
Ai	22.55	3.51	23.07	3.53	23.65	3.88	23.07	3.60
Ie	39.05	4.83	40.83	5.00	39.15	4.58	39.82	4.84
Py	12.09	2.86	13.27	2.68	12.90	2.36	12.81	2.66
Fx	10.64	4.26	11.17	3.27	13.35	4.16	11.61	3.95
Fe	21.73	4.08	21.43	4.04	21.80	4.42	21.63	4.11

*N = 22.
**N = 30.
†N = 20.
‡N = 72.

Table 10-8.
Univariate *F*-tests with (2, 69) Degrees of Freedom for Level of Existence

Source of Variation	*Sum of Squares*	*Mean Squares*	F
Do	8.26	4.13	n.s.
Cs	53.51	26.75	n.s.
Sy	185.04	92.52	4.39*
Sp	706.41	353.21	10.00**
Sa	194.19	97.09	8.11**
Wb	9.58	4.79	n.s.
Re	431.94	215.97	14.88**
So	82.91	41.46	n.s.
Sc	476.64	238.32	4.76*
To	33.68	16.84	n.s.
Gi	319.11	159.56	4.35*
Cm	3.78	1.89	n.s.
Ac	22.52	11.26	n.s.
Ai	12.78	6.39	n.s.
Ie	52.98	26.49	n.s.
Py	17.79	8.90	n.s.
Fx	87.30	43.65	n.s.
Fe	1.94	.97	n.s.
Within	25,122.64	364.12	n.s.

*$p < .05$.
**$p < .01$.

For ease of comparison, the essential data from Tables 10-8 through 10-11 have been collapsed into Table 10-12.

Examination of these data shows that the results obtained by the first univariate analysis, which includes all representatives in the sample at Graves's levels 4 through 6, were supported by the latter analysis, which included only closed personality type representatives of those levels. Notably, the variable *Sy* which was significant in the first univariate analysis, lost significance in the second one, while gains in significance were shown by variables *Wb, So,* and *Fe*. Additionally, variable *Fx*, which only approached significance over the entire sample, did achieve sig-

Table 10-9.
Univariate Analysis of Variance A Priori Contrasts

Variate	*Specified Contrasts (hypotheses)*		*Obtained Contrasts (results)*		t
Sp	5	4	5	4	−3.92*
Sa	5	4	5	4	−4.15*
Re	4	5	4	5	5.72*
Sc	4	5	4	5	2.54**
To	6	4	6	4	n.s.
Ac	4	6	4	6	n.s.
Fx	6	4	6	4	n.s.
Fe	6	5	6	5	n.s.

*$p < .01$.
**$p < .05$.

Table 10-10
Univariate *F*-tests with (2, 12) Degrees of Freedom for Closed Personality Types at Levels 4, 5, and 6

Source of Variation	*Sum of Squares*	*Mean Squares*	F
Do	14.40	7.20	n.s.
Cs	2.13	1.07	n.s.
Sy	44.80	22.40	n.s.
Sp	326.53	163.27	7.69*
Sa	65.20	32.60	6.61**
Wb	60.40	30.20	5.63**
Re	352.93	176.47	17.95*
So	102.53	51.27	6.96*
Sc	846.53	423.27	15.85*
To	40.53	20.27	n.s.
Gi	606.40	303.20	13.93*
Cm	12.93	6.47	n.s.
Ac	55.60	27.80	n.s.
Ai	29.73	14.87	n.s.
Ie	4.13	2.07	n.s.
Py	8.13	4.07	n.s.
Fx	112.53	56.27	5.10*
Fe	188.40	94.20	7.46**
Within	2,457.00	204.83	

*$p < .01$.
**$p < .05$.

Table 10-11.
Univariate Analysis of Variance A Priori Contrasts for Closed Personality Types at Levels 4, 5, and 6

Variate	*Specified Contrasts (hypotheses)*		*Obtained Contrasts (results)*		t
Sp	5	4	5	4	−3.93*
Sa	5	4	5	4	−3.03**
Re	4	5	4	5	5.73*
Sc	4	5	4	5	4.72*
To	6	4	6	4	n.s.
Ac	4	6	4	6	n.s.
Fx	6	4	6	4	−2.60**
Fe	6	5	6	5	−3.47*

*$p < .01$.
**$p < .05$.

nificance in the analysis involving only pure subsets. These statistical gains and losses may have been due, at least in part, to the lack of power of the second one-way analysis because of the small cell sizes; and it would therefore be inappropriate to overgeneralize these findings beyond stating that the results of the second analysis were largely consistent with the results of the first.

Hypothesis Summary

The results may now be summarized by applying them to the study's hypotheses (only the results of the full-sample analyses are used in this summary):

Hypothesis 1—Supported. People who were classified within a given level were more alike in their CPI responding than were people who were classified at different levels.

Hypothesis 2—Supported. On a measure of responsibility, level-4 individuals did achieve significantly higher scores than those achieved by level-5 people.

Table 10-12.
Comparison of Univariate *F*-tests and A Priori Contrasts for Total Sample and Closed Personality Types at Levels, 4, 5, and 6

Variate	F*	F**	*Specified Contrasts (hypotheses)*	*Obtained Contrasts (results)**	t	*Obtained Contrasts (results)***	t
Do	n.s.	n.s.					
Cs	n.s.	n.s.					
Sy	4.39†	n.s.					
Sp	10.00‡	7.69‡	5 > 4	5 > 4	−3.92‡	5 > 4	−3.93‡
Sa	8.11‡	6.61‡	5 > 4	5 > 4	−4.15‡	5 > 5	−3.03†
Wb	n.s.	5.63†					
Re	14.88‡	17.95‡	4 > 5	4 > 5	5.72‡	4 > 5	5.73‡
So	n.s.	6.96‡					
Sc	4.76†	15.85‡	4 > 5	4 > 5	2.54†	4 > 5	4.72‡
To	n.s.	n.s.	6 > 4	6 > 4	n.s.	6 > 4	n.s.
Gi	4.35†	13.93‡					
Cm	n.s.	n.s.					
Ac	n.s.	n.s.	4 > 6	4 > 6	n.s.	4 > 6	n.s.
Ai	n.s.	n.s.					
Te	n.s.	n.s.					
Py	n.s.	n.s.					
Fx	n.s.	5.10†	6 > 4	6 > 4	n.s.	6 > 4	−2.60†
Fe	n.s.	7.46‡	6 > 5	6 > 5	n.s.	6 > 5	−3.47‡

*n = 72.
**n = 15.
†$p < .05$.
‡$p < .01$.

Hypothesis 3—Supported. On a measure of self-control, level-4 individuals did achieve significantly higher scores than those achieved by level-5 people.

Hypothesis 4—Not Supported. No significant differences were found in a comparison of the scores achieved by level-4 and level-6 individuals on a measure of achievement via conformance.

Hypothesis 5—Supported. On a measure of social presence, level-5 individuals did achieve significantly higher scores than those achieved by level-4 individuals.

Hypothesis 6—Supported. On a measure of self-acceptance, level-5 individuals did achieve significantly higher scores than those achieved by level-4 individuals.

Hypothesis 7—Not Supported. No significant differences were found in a comparison of the scores achieved by level-4 and level-6 individuals on a measure of tolerance.

Hypothesis 8—Not Supported. No significant differences were found in a comparison of the scores achieved by level-4 and level-6 individuals on a measure of flexibility.

Hypothesis 9—Not Supported. No significant differences were found in a comparison of the scores achieved by level-5 and level-6 individuals on a measure of femininity.

Informal Descriptive Comparisons

Using the results obtained in tests of the study's hypotheses of mean differences and Gough's (1968) descriptions for the elevations of CPI scores on the significant variables, the following characterizations of Graves's levels 4 through 6 emerge:

Level 4—Saintly/Conformist. These individuals are compliant, conforming, less likely than some to force themselves upon others, and are prone to be hesitant and uncertain in social actions and interactions. They tend to be cautious, reserved, conventional, serious, submissive, sometimes prudish, often timid, and narrow in interests. In addition, they are self-denying, shy, and often discontented with their status. Stability, responsibility, reliability, dependability, and thoroughness are all valued by this group, and their behavior is dominated by overcontrol, suppression of impulse, and the restraint of individuality. They have a deeply internalized appreciation for structure and organization, and therefore they tend to be autocratic, rigid, and intolerant of differing opinions. Furthermore, saintly/conformist people are determined, organized, planful, practical, stubborn, and self-punishing.

Level 5—Materialistic. Individuals at this level may be characterized as adventurous, pleasure-seeking, self-confident, sharp-witted, unconventional, and uninhibited. They like to be with other people, but they tend to use or to manipulate them, and to take pleasure in planning and carrying out clever onslaughts against their companions' defenses. They are demanding, egotistical, opportunistic, and somewhat indifferent to others, often displaying arrogance, sarcasm, irresponsibility, and mischievousness. They are daring people who are a bit undercontrolled and quick to respond to frustration and annoyance, and they tend to react aggressively to threat or interference.

Level 6—Sociocentric. Sociocentric people may be described as humanitarian, forgiving, generous, informal, softhearted, thoughtful, and tactful, although they are somewhat idealistic and sometimes rebellious. They are flexible, adaptable, sociable, and individualistic people who are easygoing, appreciative, warm, nurturant, sympathetic, and sensitive, although they are also prone to be somewhat fickle and to have a changeable temperament.

Discussion

The similarity of these descriptions to those offered by Graves is striking, although the former lack the breadth and depth of the latter because of the limited number of CPI scales that were interpreted. Neither do the scale score interpretations offered here take into account the interactive effects of the various CPI scales, since such an in-depth analysis was not an objective of this study and would constitute an entirely different but nonetheless appropriate and recommended follow-up project. In spite of the evidence presented in this study that shows support for many of Graves's assertions about human nature, an accounting is in order for those predictions that were not upheld.

Hypothesis 4, that level-4 individuals would score higher than level-6 people on a measure of achievement via conformance, was supported directionally ($\bar{X}$ = 29.05 and $\bar{X}$ = 27.60, respectively) but failed the test of significance. The stronger showing by saintly/conformist people (relative to their level-6 counterparts) may have been a reflection of those portions of the *Ac* scale intended to indicate a "deeply internalized appreciation of structure and organization" (Gough, 1968, p. 15), a conjecture that might gain support if deeper levels of analysis were performed on the data. Further study of the *Ac* scale performed subsequent to the analysis, however, showed the scale to have been an inappropriate selection for diagnosing heightened degrees of conformity, which was this author's central criterion in selecting the scale. In Gough's words, " 'conformity' would be too strong [a term] and would also connote a kind of unproductive stereotype that is in fact not strongly embodied in the scale" (1975, p. 15). In light of the stated purpose of the *Ac* scale, though, coupled with the other reported attributes of level-4 individuals, the strong showing of these people on the scale would not be deemed out of character.

Hypothesis 7 predicted higher scores for level-6 people than for level-4 people on a measure of tolerance. It is puzzling that statistical significance was not reached by this variable, even though sociocentric people did achieve higher scores than did saintly/conformist individuals ($\bar{X}$ = 23.80 and $\bar{X}$ = 22.05, respectively). "The *To* scale was constructed as a subtle or indirect measure of the authoritarian pesonality syndrome assessed directly by the well-known California F-scale (Adorno, Frenkel-Brunswick, Levinson, & Sanford, 1950) . . . [and] is intended to reflect benign, progressive, and humanitarian sentiments at one end versus feelings of hostility, estrangement, and disbelief at the other. The typical correlation of *To* with the F-scale is −.50" (Gough, 1968, p. 13). While it is likely that saintly/conformist people do not necessarily characterize the latter-stated end of the continuum, all the literature reviewed indicated that sociocentric individuals should have closely approximated the humanitarian end of the continuum. It is possible that sociocentrics may not be as passive, good-natured, and unselfish as has heretofore been believed.

Hypothesis 8, predicting higher scores for level-6 people than for level 4's on a measure of flexibility, was also not supported. This was another puzzling result, since level-4 individuals have been characterized as "rigid" and sociocentrics as "adaptable." The hypothesis was based on the assumption that these two terms constituted the poles of a continuum, which was supported by Gough's (1968) writings on the scale. Not considered until well into the project though was Gough's interpretation that very high *Fx* scores are indicative of a "mercurial, too volatile temperament" (p. 19), a characteristic not attributed to sociocentrics by experts on Graves's theory. It was interesting to note that the variable did approach significance across the total sample of levels 4 through 6, and that it became significant ($p < .05$) over the scores of the pure subsets. This general trend favors cautious optimism about Graves's other ideas regarding sociocentrics.

The final hypothesis (9) contended that level-6 individuals would achieve higher scores than level-5 people on a measure of femininity. Regardless of the directional accuracy of the hypothesis ($\bar{X} = 21.80$ and $\bar{X} = 21.43$, respectively), statistical significance was approached but not achieved. While this outcome was initially vexing because of the similarity of the polar descriptions offered by Gough to those offered by Graves, it later began to make some sense when viewed in tandem with the results obtained for the variable *To*. Although practically no intercorrelation exists between the two scales (Gough, 1975), the *Fe* results might be interpreted to be corroborative of the *To* results; that is, some major misconceptions may be present about the nature of sociocentric people. Another possible inference is that this result supports public views that have been espoused in recent years, which indicates that those traits traditionally viewed as feminine are becoming more widely acceptanced and acknowledged by men in our culture, and that being warm, sensitive, and caring does not run counter to being masculine. The stronger showing of the variable over the pure subsets ($p < .01$) did prove problematic in light of the previous conjecture until the raw data were examined. Besides being part of a very small-sized cell, all of the randomly selected representatives of subgroup Prototype were men. This disclosure could easily be hypothesized about and discussed extensively, but for the present purpose suffice it to say that lower *Fe* scores are associated with masculinity; and it therefore seems reasonable that a greater variance would be expected between the scores of an all-male group and one that was not so constituted (the sex ratio of subset Stereotype [level-6 closed personality types] favored females, 3:2).

The last of the hypotheses was the only one that contrasted levels 5 and 6 primarily because of difficulties encountered in specifying predictions about CPI scale score differences for these groups that could be expected to be both theoretically consistent and empirically demonstrable. This uncertainty was highlighted throughout the data analysis by a consistent lack of extraordinary distinguishability between these two groups of people. Time and again the analyses produced relatively straightforward contrasts between levels 4 and 5 and between levels 4 and 6. To the end, the materialistic/sociocentric differentiation by CPI scale scores proved to be the most difficult. Since the factor analysis did confirm the distinctiveness of these levels, further studies of their CPI data are planned in an attempt to lend greater definition to the differences between materialistic and sociocentric people.

Summary

In summary, then, the results of this study are largely supportive of the level of existence point of view. The subjects who were classified according to Graves's guidelines formed three distinct homogeneous groups whose members described themselves in terms very similar to those used by Graves. These descriptions served to differentiate the levels one from the other both theoretically and empirically, and it was demonstrated that the theory's developmental claims are worthy of consideration.

Conclusions

The causal-comparative design employed in this study necessitates the exercise of caution in formulating conclusions. By definition, such designs preclude manipulative control over variables of interest (Borg & Gall, 1979), and this necessarily gives rise to the inability to rule out alternative hypotheses for the phenomenon under study (Kerlinger, 1965). The self-selection of subjects and lack of manipulative control in this research call into question the study's external validity from two separate but related standpoints.

The first of these is the generalizability of the results obtained. As noted previously, there was little evidence that the characteristics of the subjects used in this research were in any way extraordinary, and they were a fairly diverse group demoraphically. Nevertheless, initial differences were not controlled for on the basis of previous research (Rohan, 1975), and although it is not believed to have been a significant factor, the participants were similarly employed (vocationally). It remains to be demonstrated that the results produced are replicable by other samples.

The second external validity concern centers about the somewhat more global issue of the generalizability of the theory, and it is based upon the empirically documented tenet that closed people are far less prevalent than open ones. In experimental and other studies in which precise classification may assume a great deal of importance, it appears that sample sizes would have to be very large in order to find enough level exemplars to produce meaningful knowledge. From an application standpoint, however, precision may not be as much of a concern, since the major values of a level may be assumed to remain constant whether the individual is open or closed. A person who is labeled open may be viewed as more tolerant of motivation and management techniques that are not idiosyncratically appropriate for them. But in order to avoid communicating the idea that the approach is based on trial and error, consider the following example.

Based on the information gained in this study, motivation and management alternatives could be recommended to the employers of nearly 84 percent of the participants, and specific ideas and techniques could be suggested for nearly one-quarter of those. It would be very difficult to characterize this circumstance as either a trial-and-error or a shotgun approach; and while every recommendation may not be effective, the potential for successful interventions is enhanced by the absence of recommendations (based on the theory) that have little chance for success. For example, regardless of whether a person is open or closed at level 6, the use of hard-nosed authoritarian or aggressive and power-oriented approaches would be inappropriate. The point is that the theory is believed to enable the generation of numerous, fairly specific alternatives for dealing with people, and that may be its strongest recommendation for further investigation.

Further investigations, however, will almost certainly be affected by another discovery of this research: There is a need for a new instrument or some combination of existing instruments that can more clearly distinguish and discriminate among Graves's levels. In the literature surveyed, studies that designate a classification instrument, specify its scoring guidelines, and publish the results of its employment, as was done here, are rare to nonexistent. It is concluded from the experience of this study that, while there is now reason to believe that the TIB can be used reliably to classify people according to Graves's tenets, there is also evidence that the test may not be a very powerful one. Representatives of only four of Graves's levels were identified, and the data from one of these groups (level 7) were excluded from the analyses because of their extremely low incidence. The three groups that were analyzed conformed substantially to Graves's expectations, but there remains the question of the accuracy of his assertions regarding those levels not represented in this study (i.e., levels 1, 2, 3, and 8). Even though theoretically based, a priori conjectures were offered for these absences from representation, it remains to be shown that the TIB addresses concerns central to those groups, or that they are even testable by conventional means and instruments (because of Graves's descriptions of their value systems, central life concerns, and their concomitant behavioral patterns). Indeed, the identification and assessment of these groups remains as a much needed focus for future research.

An additional concern about the use of the TIB in studies of Graves's theory arose from discussions with the raters who performed the classification task. The raters believed that the fine discriminations that were sometimes necessary for accurate classification were made possible only by considerable theoretical expertise. This poses, therefore, an obstacle to replication and other types of future research that, although not insurmountable, certainly acts to impede the course of productive inquiry. Until some more widely utilitarian method for accomplishing the classification task is innovated, however, further research potential appears to rest with those who are sufficiently expert on Graves's theory to employ TIB. That, perhaps more than any other factor, may dictate the real generalizability of the theory, and it is possible that the lack of an adequate measure may be responsible for the theory's relative obscurity.

One innovation of this research that has great potential for generalization is the procedure used to test the homogeneity hypothesis and its implications for researching other "stage" theories. The procedure was based on the simple premise that if people are grouped in some way (other than pure randomization, of course), there must be some criterion on which the groupings are based. Different stage theories specify different criteria (e.g., Piaget's stages of cognitive development, Kohlberg's stages of moral development, Erikson's developmental crises), but it seems reasonable to expect that people within stages should be more alike than people between stages, regardless of the particular dimension or set of dimensions on which a theory concentrates. The *G* index of agreement (Holley, 1964; Holley & Guilford, 1964) is an easily managed statistic that quite directly addresses the testing of this homogeneity hypothesis, common to stage theories. It then makes possible the systematic investigation of other aspects of stage theories, such as examination of the discreteness of the stages, examination of the similarities and differences that define the stages, and testing of assertions regarding the developmental sequencing of the stages. If for no other reason, the procedure recommends itself from the standpoint of economical investment of research time and effort; but in this study, it also enabled the conclusion that the sample was characterized by something very similar to what Graves had described.

Whether, as Graves suggests, the groups in this project formed around a set of values, a set of needs, what was thought, or the way it was thought, or whether the subjects' common bonds were factors that remain unidentified, cannot now be accurately stated. The fact that they were constituted, and along predictable lines, is sufficient justification for more extensive study of the theory.

But all research efforts necessarily specify a reliable classification system as prerequisite which, of course, returns us to the need for a theoretically consistent categorization tool. Without it, the levels of existence point of view may well become just another theory that falls short of its academic promise.

REFERENCES

Behling, O., & Shapiro, M. B. Motivation theory: Source of solution or part of problem? *Business World*, February 1974, pp. 59–66.

Borg, W. R., & Gall, M. D. *Educational research* (3rd ed.). New York: Longman, Inc., 1979.

Flowers, V. S., & Hughes, C. L. *Value systems analysis: Study guide with supplementary readings*. Dallas, Tex: Center for Values Research, 1976.

Gellerman, W. *Management by motivation*. Binghamton, NY: Vail-Ballou Press, Inc., 1968.

Gough, H. G. *CPI: an interpreter's syllabus*. Palo Alto, Ca: Consulting Psychologists Press, Inc., 1968.

Gough, H. G. *Manual for the California Psychological Inventory*. Palo Alto, Ca: Consulting Psychologists Press, Inc., 1975.

Harman, H. *Modern Factor Analysis.* Chicago: University of Chicago Press, 1968.

Hazlett, R. L. Levels of existence: A values-based approach to human motivation and management (doctoral dissertation, University of Virginia, 1980). *Dissertation Abstracts International,* 1980, *41*, Ref. #3617B. (University Microfilm No. 80-27953)

Holley, J. W. A reply to some comments of Norman Cliff. *Educational and Psychological Measurement,* 1964, *24*(2), 313–317.

Holley, J. W., & Guilford, J. P. A note on the G index of agreement. *Educational and Psychological Measurement,* 1964, **24**(2), 749–753.

Kerlinger, F. N. *Foundations of behavioral research.* New York: Holt, Rinehart and Winston, 1965.

Rohan, T. M. Should a worker's personality affect your managing? *Industry Week,* May 5, 1975, pp. 28–38.

INDEX